MW00782693

Using RTI in Secondary Schools

Thanks for your valuable Contribution to this Book. I am forever grateful.

— Wayn

This book is dedicated to educators who work tirelessly on behalf of struggling students. Your heart, art, and professionalism make an immeasurable difference.

On behalf of society, thank you.

Using RTI in Secondary Schools

A Training Manual for Successful Implementation

Wayne A. Callender

CORWIN
A SAGE Company

FOR INFORMATION:

Corwin

A SAGE Company

2455 Teller Road

Thousand Oaks, California 91320

(800) 233-9936

www.corwin.com

SAGE Publications Ltd.

1 Oliver's Yard

55 City Road

London EC1Y 1SP

United Kingdom

SAGE Publications India Pvt. Ltd.

B 1/I 1 Mohan Cooperative Industrial Area

Mathura Road, New Delhi 110 044

India

SAGE Publications Asia-Pacific Pte. Ltd.

3 Church Street

#10-04 Samsung Hub

Singapore 049483

Copyright © 2014 by Corwin

All rights reserved. When forms and sample documents are included, their use is authorized only by educators, local school sites, and/or noncommercial or nonprofit entities that have purchased the book. Except for that usage, no part of this book may be reproduced or utilized in any form or by any means, electronic or mechanical, including photocopying, recording, or by any information storage and retrieval system, without permission in writing from the publisher.

Printed in the United States of America

A catalog record of this book is available from the Library of Congress.

ISBN 978-1-4522-9056-0

This book is printed on acid-free paper.

Executive Editor: Arnis Burvikovs

Associate Editor: Ariel Price

Production Editor: Amy Schroller

Copy Editor: Deanna Noga

Typesetter: C&M Digitals (P) Ltd.

Proofreader: Dennis W. Webb

Indexer: Scott Smiley

Cover Designer: Janet Kiesel

Marketing Manager: Amanda Boudria

14 15 16 17 18 10 9 8 7 6 5 4 3 2 1

Contents

List of Acronyms

Publisher's Acknowledgments

Corwin gratefully acknowledges the contributions of the following reviewers:

Maria Banks, Corwin Author and
  Educational Consultant
Toolz4Teachers LLC
Willow Grove, PA

Dr. A. L. Hough-Everage, Professor
  of Education
Brandman University
Victorville, CA

Chris Hubbuch, Principal
Excelsior Springs Middle School
Excelsior Springs, MO

Ronda Mitchell, Director/Assistant
  Professor
University of Illinois at Springfield
Springfield, IL

Dr. Sylvia Rockwell, Assistant
  Professor
Saint Leo University
Ocala, FL

Dr. Judith A. Rogers, K-5 Math
  Specialist
Tucson Unified School District
Tucson, AZ

Erin Schons, M.S. SPED
Assistant Education Director
Children's Home Society
Sioux Falls, SD

Cara Shores, Educational
  Consultant, Corwin Author
Wesley Educational Services
Taylorsville, GA

Dr. Janet Slowman Chee, School
  Psychologist
Waterflow, NM

About the Author

 **Wayne Callender** is a national RTI Consultant who has worked at the state, district, and building levels. He is a former statewide RTI Director and currently trains and advises educators across the country in the implementation of systems for school improvement. In addition to being featured as keynote speaker at over a dozen state and national conferences, Wayne spends significant time working directly with districts and schools establishing schoolwide RTI structures. Wayne is the President of Partners for Learning, Inc. located in Boise, Idaho.

Introduction 1

Consider this scenario. You are a junior high school science teacher. It is late October and a new student enters your classroom. Without the benefit of information from previous schooling, you are left hoping this is a student with the essential prerequisite reading and math skills to be successful in your classroom. Within several days you become concerned. The student appears to be struggling, is not completing work, and is reluctant to ask for assistance. You refer the student to the school's student assistant team by completing prereferral paperwork. The student assistant team meets and recommends the student attend afterschool tutoring and that teachers allow additional time for the student to complete assignments. By early December, the team meets to review the student's status. Because the student is still having difficulties, the team recommends the student be evaluated for special education. Although referrals to special education typically occur in elementary school, referrals at the secondary level often reflect limited viable options for struggling students; despite referrals, very few learning disabilities are diagnosed in middle and high school. The school contacts the parents to obtain permission for an evaluation. After winter break the evaluation begins. The evaluation process is completed in five weeks. An eligibility meeting is held mid-February. Based on the assessment results, the student is found ineligible for Special Education Services because skill deficits are not severe enough to qualify as having a specific learning disability. End result . . . the student continues to struggle as teachers do their best to provide support within the classroom. By the end of the semester the student fails three classes.

Now imagine another scenario. The same student enrolls late October to your school—a school with an RTI support structure already in place. In this school, the student upon enrolling was administered a brief reading, writing, and math screener to assess academic skills. On completion of the screeners, the student then shadows a classmate to learn about the schools policies, meet peers, and become comfortable with the building. By the end of the first day, the screening results are scored and reviewed with the student and the student's parents. The screening indicates the student's reading and writing skills are far below grade level. As a result, the student is administered a diagnostic placement test to confirm the screening results and to determine what interventions and placement will best meet his or her needs. The student is then scheduled into a reading/writing intervention class where he or she will receive research validated interventions for one class period per day. Eleven other students are already in this reading intervention class, all with like reading difficulties and similar instructional needs. In addition to an intervention class, the student is assigned an adult mentor and provided information regarding the before and after school tutoring program where students can receive general support in all content area classes. By the end of the semester, the student, as a result of direct interventions, has greatly improved his or her reading and writing skills. Afterschool support has provided both incentive and assistance, allowing the student to be successful in all classes. Most important, the student is passing all his or her classes. By the end of the year, intervention may no longer be necessary, although it could be provided for multiple years if required.

Now, which scenario would you prefer in your school? Which school would you prefer to work in as a teacher? Most important, which system would you prefer for your own middle or high school aged student?

School A:

- Student given a class schedule without screening prerequisite academic skills in reading, writing, and math.
- School waits for records.
- Teacher identifies a concern and then requests assistance for the student.
- Two weeks later, prereferral is initiated.
- Prereferral process completed in December.
- Student is recommended for evaluation for special education.
- Parental consent is obtained.
- Evaluation initiated in January.
- Evaluation complete and eligibility meeting held end of February.
- Student is found ineligible for services as discrepancy requirements are not met.
- Student fails three classes second semester.

School B:

- Student screened as part of enrollment process.
- Screening results are reviewed with student and the student's parents.

- Screening indicates the student is a candidate for intervention in reading and writing.
- The student is given a placement test to determine instructional placement.
- Student is placed in class for reading and writing interventions.
- Student is placed in appropriate intervention the day of enrollment.
- The student is provided an adult mentor and content area tutoring via before and after school programs.

In simple terms, Response to Intervention (RTI) can be a practical, research-based approach to helping students who struggle. It can and should be capable of providing to all students necessary support such as the scenario described for the student in School B. Central to a systems approach to RTI is that students in need of support and/or intervention receive it. A key concept to systems RTI is that teachers are not left to "figure it out." Rather, a system is in place that is supportive of students and teachers.

Unfortunately, the scenario described in School B is in fact the exception rather than the rule for many secondary schools. Too often, intervention occurs late, is fragmented, and is not specific to the skill deficits of the student. Too often, intervention is not supported by the system as a whole. Indeed, struggling students and the educators who support them face long odds of achieving academic improvement as a result of the traditional practices in secondary schools.

WHY RTI?

Why is RTI critical in secondary education?

CONSIDER . . .

- Eighty-five percent of all juveniles who come into contact with the juvenile court system are functionally illiterate.

- Sixty percent of all prison inmates are functionally illiterate, 75 percent of inmates are illiterate at the twelfth-grade level, and 19 percent are completely illiterate.

- Inmates have a 16 percent chance of returning to prison if they receive literacy help, as opposed to 70 percent for those who receive no help.

(Rosario, 2010)

According to the Consortium on Chicago School Research (Allensworth & Easton, 2005), who developed an "on-track indicator" that correlates dropping out of high school with class failure, failing one semester class during the freshman year decreases the likelihood of graduating from 80 percent to 63 percent. Failing two semester classes decreases the likelihood to 44 percent. Fail three semester classes all but assures a student will exit before graduation—only 31 percent chance of graduating. Dropping out of high school would not be so alarming if students were successful once they leave. Contrary to occasional stories of a successful dropout, the overwhelming majority of students who do not complete high school face limited options for meaningful, long-term employment and a life path very different from their educated peers.

WHO DROPS OUT?

Students with long histories of underachievement drop out disproportionately. Reading is key. According to U.S. Department of Education (2010), more than 60 percent of middle and high school students scored below proficient in reading, meaning the majority of such students do not possess the essential reading skills necessary to pass content area classes at the secondary level.

- Every year nearly 3,030,000 students drop out of school. That's 8,300 students per day.
- Seventy-five percent of crime is committed by high school dropouts.

(Education Week, Children Trends Database, January 1, 2014)

Illiteracy and crime are closely related. The Department of Justice states, "The link between academic failure and delinquency, violence, and crime is *welded to reading failure.*"

- Over 70 percent of inmates in America's prisons cannot read above a fourth-grade level.

APPROACHES TO ADDRESSING STRUGGLING STUDENTS—WHAT HAPPENED IN ELEMENTARY SCHOOL?

Because many schools don't have structures in place to implement necessary interventions, most teachers end up isolated and left to their own devices when trying to help students who struggle.

Historically, the most common approaches to help struggling students at the elementary level are the following:

Approach A	*Approach B*	*Approach C*
The student receives additional assistance with grade-level work—that is, tutoring, extra help, preferential seating, and so on.	The student is referred for testing to identify potential learning problems, abilities, strengths, and weaknesses.	The student is served through remedial services or special education.

The above three approaches, unfortunately, do not have a good track record in bringing about meaningful, long-term improvement in the student's performance; they are typically delayed, provided inconsistently, and not targeted specifically to the student's skill deficits. In fact, Approach C—qualifying a student for special and remedial education services, often seen as the goal for testing students in the first place—more often reflects compliance with regulatory policies than alignment with best practices for improving academic outcomes.

In an effort to prevent unnecessary evaluations and placement into special education, the prereferral system has historically been utilized by schools across the United States. The objective of prereferral is to provide intervention plans that will help students succeed in the regular classroom. However well intended, prereferral has been largely a failure; it did not reduce the number of students evaluated and identified for special education. In fact, there is little empirical evidence that most prereferral processes, whether at the elementary or secondary level, resulted in better outcomes for students (Flugum & Reschly, 1994). For most educators familiar with prereferral, such findings are not a shocking revelation.

Like their elementary counterparts, secondary schools often lack a coherent, efficient plan for identifying and providing intervention to students in need. A possible explanation for the ineffectiveness of educational systems may rest with the structures of schools themselves. Interventions most often take the form of a series of strategies, such as those identified in Approach A. Without a systematic procedure for carrying out intensive, targeted, and sustained interventions, teachers have little hope of addressing all but minor and easily fixed problems—the kind not necessarily related to long-term academic failure. In most instances, secondary systems do not provide teachers with necessary resources or supports beyond those already available within their classrooms.

YOUR TURN

OVERVIEW—ACTIVITY 1

As a team

1. Think of a student(s) you have known with academic skill deficits. Identify the student(s).
2. What specific interventions were provided to the student? How long were they carried out?
3. What was the outcome for the student (for example, was reading comprehension improved?).
4. Discuss the effectiveness of your school/district's system or plan for addressing secondary students with skill deficits.

An RTI Approach for Secondary Schools

Two popular approaches to RTI include (1) a standard protocol approach and (2) a problem-solving approach. Schools using a standard protocol approach identify prescribed procedures, assessments, and interventions for students in need of academic and behavioral supports. Procedures within this approach are often aligned to the three tiers, including universal interventions, targeted interventions, and intensive interventions. A problem-solving approach, in contrast, relies on a school-based team to identify specific concerns of individual students then brainstorm interventions. Struggling students in a problem-solving approach are typically addressed individually, each with a specific plan for intervention. Although tailored to specific students' needs, individual plans for intervention are often time- and resource-intensive and difficult to sustain long term, especially if there are multiple students requiring support. Such an approach is especially burdensome if the system as a whole does not become more proactive and preventative because many students will require support.

Although each approach has advantages and disadvantages, RTI, as presented in this manual, maximizes the advantages of both approaches. The result is a systems approach that includes

- a tiered intervention structure for supporting student needs, including targeted and intensive interventions that are research validated and matched to student specific skill deficits;

- supports that do not require students to "qualify" are immediate and provided long term as necessary;
- maximizing the use of all existing resources, including general and special education, for the benefit of all students;
- assessment for the purpose of instructional decision making (screening, diagnostic, and progress monitoring);
- adopting general classroom instructional practices that are based on scientific research; and
- engaging in problem solving to address concerns at the systems, group, and individual student levels.

Pre and Post RTI

The contrast between the traditional, process-driven approach and the new outcome-driven approach represents a fundamental shift in thinking about how we view student problems and the school's role in addressing these problems. Note the differences in the table below.

Pre RTI	Post RTI
Learning problems are often a sign of a disability.	Learning problems are a breakdown in the instructional process, that is, interaction among instruction, curriculum, environment, and learner.
Test to confirm or rule out a disability.	Assess to identify what needs to be taught and inform instruction.
Delivery of service (remedial or special education).	Improve performance (skill emphasis) and enable learning.

Why the change in approaches? Using the process-driven model, attention was too often devoted to procedural-driven practices that may or may not lead to improved student outcomes. Some flaws with traditional approaches were that

- They emphasized adherence to regulatory policies rather than effective instructional practices.
- Assessments produced too much unnecessary information and too little usable information, such as what to teach and the best way of teaching it.

- Educators were taught to look for complex explanations for learning problems rather than being trained how to collect and use diagnostic information to address validated skill deficits.
- Many students fell through the cracks as a result of having to qualify for services or received ineffective or delayed intervention even when they did qualify.

THE NEED FOR A SYSTEMIC APPROACH

The shortcomings of efforts to support struggling students at the secondary level, including special education, have been well documented. Secondary schools are often not structured to meet the needs of students who are not proficient. This creates a perilous position for any one teacher or any particular program such as special education. As a result, regular education itself must be structured to meet the needs of students who routinely walk through the door with academic and behavioral deficits. This requires a proactive structure where interventions are available without delay for any students who need them—no qualifying necessary. In such a structure, student instructional needs are identified through universal screening (often simply using existing assessments such as MAP or state testing) and functional academic assessments (used for diagnostic purposes), interventions are matched to instructional needs of students, and schools are structured to provide what students need by using all available resources within the building.

Developing systems in secondary schools requires:

1. Support services be redefined and aligned to student instructional needs. The table below illustrates the various levels of student needs. Note: Each level described can be applied to particular areas such as Language Arts and Math. For instance, students could be Benchmark in Language Arts (LA) and Intensive in Math.

Level of Support	Definition	Implications for Instruction
Advanced	Students above grade level; at or above the 75th percentile	Opportunities for challenge and curriculum advancement
Benchmark	Students at grade level and low risk for academic failure; at or above the 40th percentile	Proactive and preventive; effective instruction designed to maximize learning outcomes

Level of Support	Definition	Implications for Instruction
Strategic	Students 1–2 years below grade level; between the 20th and 39th percentile; at risk for failure	Targeted supports in addition to the core instruction
Intensive	Students significantly below grade level in areas such as reading. Most often 2 or more grade levels below and below the 20th percentile	Intensive supports that accelerate learning in the key skill

2. Paradigm Shift

   We must change our way of thinking about education by

   - Recognizing that secondary schools must have interventions and supports to address students with skill deficits
   - Using assessments that identify what students need and evaluate effectiveness of instruction
   - Identifying reasons students struggle; defining the problem in instructional terms
   - Altering our view of solutions to secondary student problems (intervention vs. content area support, regular education ownership vs. special education responsibility)
   - Changing our expectations for intervention from procedurally driven to solution oriented

3. Professional Development

   We must provide professional development for all educators and parents, by

   - Providing training in instructional leadership to principals and district office administrators
   - Providing training and coaching to teachers using intervention programs
   - Providing training and coaching in effective instructional practices to all teachers and instructional staff
   - Providing training to related service groups (consultants, psychologists, social workers, speech pathologists) on involvement in a systems approach
   - Including training and supports for parents and guardians

4. Administrative and Policy Support
   We must support a well-designed structure by

   - Ensuring that school administrators are trained on how to organize and support effective structures, including curriculum, instruction, and environments
   - Advocating that building and district resource decisions are based on student needs and performance data
   - Providing administrative leadership and support of data-based decision making
   - Developing policy to support the use of student outcomes as the measure of effective systems and as a means of determining program efficacy

From Theory to Practice

To make the big ideas of RTI workable and sustainable, we need a protocol for addressing the needs of all students. Assessment should identify students in need, inform instruction, and evaluate student progress and program effectiveness. Instruction must be scientifically validated and include teaching practices that have been demonstrated to be highly effective for students to which they are applied. Problem solving for systems and individuals must be an integral part of the structure.

RTI Core Beliefs

One danger of educational change, particularly at the secondary level, is that we begin with a vision of what we need but end up with something that more resembles what we already had in the first place or we make very minor changes to an existing system, yet expect major results. Indeed, familiar practices and long-standing school structures are difficult to change. Change requires a clear vision, planning, time, patience, and a relentless pursuit toward achieving a culture that does not accept student failure as an option.

More than maintaining the daily practices associated with RTI, overriding goals must also be recognized and expressed to ensure we do not lose track of the RTI purpose. Although implementation may vary from school to school, RTI

- Is about improving student outcomes
- Provides support to teachers and guardians

- Allows for immediate intervention
- Focuses on alterable academic and behavioral skills and evaluates progress
- Assures no student falls between the cracks
- Seeks to solve problems rather than create placements
- Uses assessment for the purpose of instruction and decision making
- Maximizes use of all resources for the purpose of improving student outcomes

---

We have witnessed over the last 30 years numerous attempts at planned educational change. The benefits have not nearly equaled the costs, and all too often, the situation has seemed to worsen. We have, however, gained clearer and clearer insights over this period about the do's and don'ts of bringing about change. . . . **One of the most promising features of this new knowledge about change is that successful examples of innovation are based on what might be most accurately labeled "organized common sense."** (Fullan, 1991, pp. xi–xii)

SUMMARY

A Systems Approach to RTI

A well-designed structure aligns appropriate levels of supports to students at various levels, ensuring supports are highly effective. A systems approach includes the following essential components:

- A system that meets the needs of the full range of students (Benchmark, Strategic, Intensive (B, S, I)).
- Universal screening and placement of students according to instructional needs in reading, writing, math, and behavior.
- Differentiated instruction to meet the needs of instructional groups and individual students.
- Research-based interventions and instructional practices.
- Frequent progress monitoring to inform decision making.
- Ongoing professional development to support system-wide structures of instruction.
- Data used to evaluate the effectiveness of schoolwide systems and instructional effectiveness.
- Problem-solving teams to identify and address unhealthy or less effective systems.

- Intervention plans for students whose needs cannot be adequately addressed within the system; for example, for students who require intervention or instruction not available as part of the overall system.
- Applying information collected during implementation of the above components as well as the student's response to intervention for determining eligibility for special education. Such information includes
  - o progress-monitoring data,
  - o review of intervention (duration and general effectiveness for similar students),
  - o intervention quality and level of fidelity,
  - o instructor's training and level of expertise, and
  - o efforts to intensify or change interventions depending on student progress.

PURPOSE OF THE CORE TRAINING MANUAL

RTI as presented in this manual is a systematic, systems approach that uses all the resources within a building to address students with academic and behavioral difficulties.

This core training manual includes the essential components needed to implement a systematic and comprehensive Response to Intervention approach. For secondary schools, the primary focus is on the development and use of a three-tier instructional model and includes

- effective systems and structured levels of support;
- data-based decision making;
- research-based interventions; and
- problem solving for systems, groups, and individual students.

This training manual translates current educational research into practical application to help schools maximize resources and outcomes for all students.

OBJECTIVES OF THE CORE TRAINING MANUAL

Participants in the training program will

- Understand the essential components of a tiered instructional model

- Develop and evaluate the effectiveness of a three-tier instruction model
- Identify schoolwide considerations involved in student achievement and outcomes
- Establish and complete a process for universal screening
- Acquire a working knowledge of curriculum-based measurement and other progress-monitoring techniques
- Evaluate and use problem-solving techniques to improve systems efficiency and resulting outcomes for all students
- Use functional assessments to evaluate and determine instructional needs for students
- Systematically connect and use formative progress monitoring to inform instruction at the systems, group, and individual student levels
- Use functional academic assessments and problem solving to create a comprehensive student Intervention Plan (I-Plan)
- Understand the essential components of using an RTI approach to special education

RTI at the Secondary Level—A Systems Approach

2

OBJECTIVES:

- Identify the core principals of a systems approach to Response to Intervention
- Understand the design of an effective educational structure
- Develop multi-tiered support for students
- Understand the purpose and use of Placement Pathways and Intervention sequences

A systems approach to RTI is proactive and preventative, but most important, responsive to student needs. Consider your school's response to students with skill deficits or who transfer into your building in the middle of the year. How well structured is your school to identify and meet their needs? Are supports immediate and automatic? Or do they require students to first fail, then be referred for services? Are teachers left to try and meet students' needs in content classes? How much time is lost determining

> It is not the pace of change that is the culprit; it is the piecemealness and fragmentation that wears us down.
>
> —Fullan, 2003

what support will be provided, then arranging for it to begin? Consider the approach taken by the two schools in the Introduction, School A and School B, and their responses to a transfer student. Remember that it is late October when the student enrolls.

School A:

- Student given a class schedule without screening prerequisite academic skills in reading, writing, and math.
- School waits for records.
- Teacher identifies a concern.
- Two weeks later, prereferral is initiated.
- Prereferral process completed in December.
- Student is recommended for evaluation.
- Parental consent is obtained.
- Evaluation initiated in January.
- Evaluation complete and eligibility meeting held end of February.
- Student is found ineligible for services.
- Student fails three classes second semester.

School B:

- Student screened as part of enrollment process.
- Screening results are reviewed with student and the student's parents.
- Screening indicates the student is a candidate for intervention in reading and writing.
- The student is given a placement test to determine initial intervention placement.
- Student is placed in class for reading and writing interventions.
- Student is placed in appropriate intervention the day of enrollment.
- The student is provided an adult mentor and content area tutoring via before and after school programs.

For many schools, early efforts with RTI involved problem solving at the individual student level. That is, students were referred to the school's team to identify and carry out interventions, and such referrals were only made after students demonstrated difficulties or were not successful in regular classes. Despite the effectiveness of this process in resolving individual student concerns, these efforts made little impact on the school as a whole. This is primarily because they failed to address larger, systemic concerns, which, left unchecked, created many of the students referred for intervention planning in the first place. Perhaps even more problematic was the attempt to address struggling kids one at a time. With this approach, a school never ran out of students for whom to problem solve.

To be successful and sustainable long term, RTI must be more than a set of interventions targeting struggling students. In fact, lessons from secondary schools with years of experience implementing RTI suggest that attention must be focused on establishing an overall effective structure, one uniquely designed to meet the needs of all students. Such a structure is differentiated to student instructional needs, from the high-achieving student to the learning disabled.

Core principles of an RTI school are

1. Use a tiered approach for addressing student needs according to risk—that is, Benchmark (low risk/skill proficient), Strategic (some risk/nonproficient), and Intensive (high risk/severe deficits).

2. Maximize the use of regular and special education resources for the benefit of all students.

3. Use assessment for the purpose of instructional decision making (that is, screening, diagnosis, and progress monitoring).

4. Adopt interventions and instructional practices that are based in scientific research (in other words—interventions that have been demonstrated to work).

5. Place emphasis on evaluating and improving system effectiveness rather than focusing solely on individual student response to intervention.

USING A TIERED APPROACH

Designing an Effective Educational Structure—Something for Everyone

At the universal or Tier 1 level, instructional practices help students be successful by incorporating effective teaching strategies in content area classes. Strong instruction in content classes benefits all students with or without skill deficits. Tier 2 and 3 supports are provided to students with specific skills deficits (such as in writing, reading, comprehension, etc.). Such supports should not require students to "qualify" but are provided in addition to content area instruction, often in special intervention classes designated for students with like instructional needs but not provided by special education or taught by special education teachers. Such intervention classes are provided through the regular secondary educational system.

A systems approach to RTI differs from a traditional three-tier model in at least two important ways: (1) in a systems approach, Tier 3 is not synonymous with special education—meaning students can receive intensive intervention regardless of whether they are in special education or not; and (2) students do not have to first receive a lower level of support (Tier 1 or Tier 2) to be tried prior to Tier 3 placement. With a systems approach, students receive the level of support that aligns with the severity of their deficits.

Tier 1 Benchmark Support: Provides grade-level, content-specific instruction.

Tier 2 Strategic Support: Provides targeted intervention and additional support for students somewhat below grade level.

Tier 3 Intensive Support: Provides supports for students who are significantly below grade level in essential skills.

Tier 1—Core Content Instruction

Students who do not have specific skill deficits in basic underlying reading, writing, and math skills fit into this category. Such students are generally at or above the 40th percentile and, as a result, are low risk for academic failure, including performance on state testing as well as performance in content area classes.

Tier 1 synonyms include: low risk, Benchmark, and proficient

Tier 1/Benchmark Instruction Provides:

- Content area, core instruction
- Instruction for the majority of students
- Aligned to grade-level standards
- Additional supports required for students to master content standards, such as reteaching, differentiation, additional time, accommodations as required for students to access content area standards

Tier 2—Strategic Instruction

Students between the 20th and 39th percentile in reading, writing, and/or math fit into this category. Tier 2/Strategic students have a questionable probability of passing state assessments and often are at risk of failing content area classes. Tier 2 students may have difficulty in the areas of motivation and persistence, which are also predictive of success and can help students overcome skill deficits.

Tier 2 synonyms include: slightly below proficient, Strategic

Tier 2/Strategic Instruction Provides:

- Additional instruction in one or more areas (targeted instruction, for example, comprehension, vocabulary, writing conventions, fractions, etc.)
- More instruction or practice in particular area(s) of need
- Additional support for initial learning
- More teacher scaffolding
- More explicit and systematic instruction
- More opportunities for practice and corrective feedback

Tier 3—Intensive

Intensive instruction is for students with severe skill deficits and who are at high risk for failure. Intensive level students are typically below the 20th percentile in a particular domain such as reading. Such students are often missing a wide array of skills and benefit from a more comprehensive and sustained intervention approach—for instance, intensive students would be placed in a reading intervention that coordinates instruction across the areas of phonics, fluency, vocabulary, and comprehension.

Tier 3 synonyms include: high risk, Intensive, significantly below

Tier 3/Intensive Instruction Provides:

- Direct and explicit learning opportunities using modeling, scaffolding, guided practice, corrective feedback
- Carefully designed instructional sequence, systematic instruction that teaches to a high criterion level of performance
- A *hear it, see it, say it, do it* format with lots of modeling and repetition for initial learning
- Ensure mastery of skills taught and provide controlled practice opportunities and transfer of skills

Logistically . . . How Do You Make a Systems or Tiered Approach Work? Mapping Out a Plan

Establishing a tiered, systematic structure in secondary schools requires significant planning. Figuring out the logistics of a schoolwide approach at the secondary level can be more difficult than (and as important as) providing the actual instruction. Without a way to make it happen, supports and well-designed interventions are of little use.

Below is an explanation of an instructional decision-making format called the Placement Pathway. Following the explanation are specific secondary math Pathways followed by examples of reading and math Pathways (see pp. 20–21). Placement Pathways are a blueprint that details a school's plan for carrying out schoolwide supports. A Placement Pathway can be established in the areas of reading, math, writing, behavior, good standing, or any area in which a protocol for decision making and action planning is necessary.

The Placement Pathway identifies

- How students are to be screened
- What criterion is used for placement in the various levels of support or tiers
- The instructional focus—what will be addressed
- What interventions or supports are to be provided
- For how long and how supports are to be delivered
- The method for evaluating student progress
- How system effectiveness will be verified

INTERVENTION SEQUENCING

Whereas the Placement Pathway is used to map out how placement decisions are made, the Intervention Sequence spells out what happens next. The Intervention Sequence identifies how interventions are aligned in sequential fashion. Where does intervention start (at instructional level) and where does it end (the exit point) and all the steps in between.

The following example of an Intervention Sequence (p. 23) shows an intervention progression using a combination of two published intervention programs, Corrective Reading and Language!. Enter and exit points are identified along with anticipated duration for each level. Students enter the sequence according to the Corrective Reading Placement Test, which aligns student skill levels to the correct program starting point. Once placed, the Intervention Sequence maps out progression from the starting point through intervention completion—the point at which students would be skill proficient and therefore exit intervention. Each level must be successfully completed to progress to the next level in the sequence. In the example, successful completion of each level is evaluated using internal assessments provided by the intervention programs as well as external assessments such as CBMs—measures of whether the student is able to transfer skills outside the program.

Example Middle School Reading Placement Pathway

Screening	INTENSIVE	INTENSIVE	STRATEGIC	STRATEGIC	STRATEGIC	STRATEGIC	STRATEGIC	BENCHMARK	ADVANCED
New students and those below 50th %ile on MAP receive EasyCBM Screening									
Diagnosis: Criteria	At or Below 10th percentile on EasyCBM all three areas (High Risk Level) (difficulty with multiple reading skills)	At/Below 10th percentile on EasyCBM PRF (Some Risk)	Between the 11th and 39th percentile on EasyCBM PRF (Some Risk) with Phonic Deficits (fast/slow & wrong)	Between the 11th and 39th percentile on EasyCBM PRF (Some Risk) Pass the Phonics Screener	At/Below 10th percentile on EasyCBM MCRC (Some Risk)	Between the 20th and 39th percentile on EasyCBM MCRC (Some Risk) (accurate and fluent, poor comprehension) Red/Yellow on Vocab	Between the 20th and 39th percentile on EasyCBM MCRC (Some Risk) (accurate and fluent, poor comprehension) Green on Vocab	Between the 20th and 39th percentile on EasyCBM (fast & right)	Above 75th percentile on EasyCBM demonstrates need for additional challenge/advancement
Focus	COMPREHENSIVE	PHONICS	PHONICS (PRF)	FLUENCY (PRF)	COMPREHENSION (MCRC)	COMPREHENSION (MCRC & VOCAB)	COMPREHENSION & Vocabulary (MCRC & VOCAB)	CORE CONTENT	ENRICHMENTS
Focus Skills	Basic reading skills: Letter/sound correspondence, decoding, fluency, vocabulary, comprehension	Letter/sound correspondence, decoding, fluency	Letter/sound correspondence, decoding, fluency	Automatically decoding words, reading high frequency, and phrasing sentences	Comprehension Skills and/or Strategies	Comprehension Skills and/or Strategies	Comprehension Skills and/or Strategies	Core Coursework	Advanced Content Focus Comprehension Strategies, Writing
Intervention	Alternate Core, Corrective Reading Decoding and Corrective Reading Comprehension	**Corrective Reading** Decoding	**Rewards**	**Fluency Solution** includes comprehension	**READ 180** includes fluency	**READ 180** includes fluency	**Read to Achieve** includes fluency	Regular Core Class	Regular Core Class, additional Enrichment class
Length of Time	Two Class Periods per day	1 class period B1/B2: 1 quarter C: 1 Semester	1 class period 1 semester	2 class periods until proficient	2 class periods until proficient	2 class periods until proficient	Semester/Year		
Verify Progress	In-Program assessments and EasyCBM (all measures)	In-Program and EasyCBM PRF						*Performance in Core Coursework *Grades	*Classroom performance *Rubrics on projects
Identify Method to Verify Effectiveness	*Percent of students making adequate progress on EasyCBM in each support category								

The above percentile ranges reflect the criteria customized by the school.

Example High School Reading Placement Pathway Plan

New students and those below below 40th %ile on MAP, receive AIMSweb (R-CBM & Maze)

Screening	Tier III INTENSIVE — Below 10th %ile on AIMS	Tier II STRATEGIC — 11th–30th %ile on the R-CBM and/or Maze			Tier I BENCHMARK — 31st–70th%ile / 41%-70th%ile	Tier I ADVANCED — 71st–99th %ile
Grade Level Assessments						
Diagnosis: Criteria	At or Below 10th percentile on R-CBM and/or Maze	Strategic level reading skills (11th – 30th percentile) as measured by MAP and AIMSweb			MAP, R-CBM, Maze and/or EasyCBM — Fast & Right	MAP, R-CBM, Maze and/or EasyCBM — Demonstrates the need for additional challenge and advancement — Fast & Right
Focus	COMPREHENSIVE	PHONICS	FLUENCY	COMPREHENSION	CORE CONTENT	ENRICHMENTS
Focus Skills	Basic reading skills: Letter/sound correspondence, decoding, fluency, vocabulary, comprehension	Targeted decoding skills	Automatically decoding words, reading high frequency, and phrasing sentences.	Comprehension skills and/or strategies	Core coursework	Advanced Content Focus Comprehension Strategies Writing
Intervention	Core Replacement: CORRECTIVE READING Decoding A, B1, B2, or C Comprehension A, B, or C or REACH HIGHER	Fusion Reading Followed by Read to Achieve (must complete Fusion Reading first) (Taught by a regular LA teacher)			Regular Core Class	Honors Classes AP Classes Dual Credit Classes
Length of Time	2 Class Periods/day (In place of regular Lang. Arts)	1 Class Period/day in addition to a Regular LA class Semester/Year			Semester/Year	Semester/Year
Verify Progress	Program assessments AIMS	Program assessments AIMS R-CBM and/or Maze			*Performance in Core coursework *Assessments *Grades	*Classroom performance *Rubrics on projects *Grades
Identify Method to Verify Effectiveness	*Percent of students making adequate progress on AIMS in each support category					

The above percentile ranges reflect the criteria customized by the school.

The Intervention Sequence provides a clear, cohesive plan for ensuring the school's interventions are aligned and students are not dropped prematurely. The path to intervention completion and exit is mapped out for everyone, including students, teachers, and parents, to see and understand. Such sequencing helps ensure interventions are logically ordered with clear outcomes identified. If a school does not have its interventions clearly sequenced out, there is a danger interventions will be a patchwork of well-intended efforts with no direction and no end, allowing students to become intervention "lifers."

AN RTI FRAMEWORK TO ENSURE SUCCESS

Differences in how schools are organized and function account to a large degree for differences in student outcomes.

Highly effective schools have

- Strong instructional leadership
- Highly skilled instructors
- High expectations of student achievement for all students
- Broadly understood instructional focus
- Measures of student achievement as a basis for program and systems evaluation
- Problem solving to improve systems as well as students
- Instructional materials appropriate for diverse secondary learners, including highly structured instructional reading, writing, and math programs
- Differentiated instruction

Of course, it is possible to have all the above features and still not have a highly effective RTI school. For a systems approach to RTI to be successful, students at risk must make meaningful and significant progress. If they are at risk, intervention efforts must, over time, move students toward proficiency and thereby reduce risk. This means instructional supports, or tiers, must be highly effective. Effective tiers mean each level is effective for the majority of students to whom it is applied. Students not progressing in an otherwise effective system can be identified, and problems can be solved at the individual student level. In contrast, supports not working for a majority of students should be identified and problem solved at the systems level illustrated on p. 25. Failure to differentiate systems versus student problems will result in a focus on students and students' characteristics rather than instructional

Reading Intervention Sequence Chart

New students that place more than 2 years below grade level on Reading Mastery placement test will be placed in Corrective Reading.

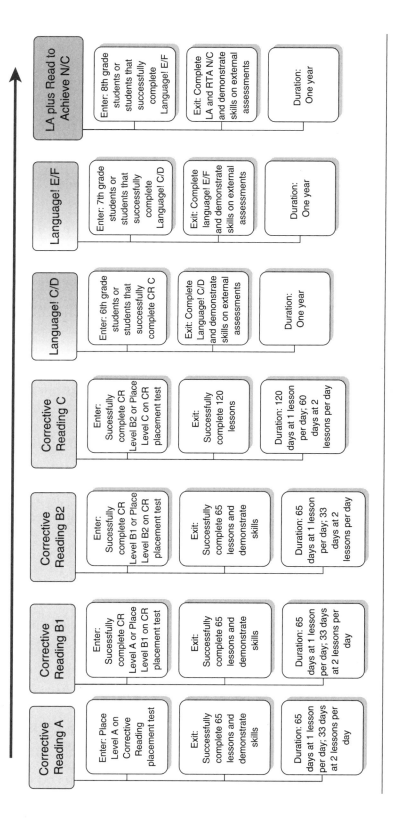

Corrective Reading A

Enter: Place Level A on Corrective Reading placement test

Exit: Successfully complete 65 lessons and demonstrate skills

Duration: 65 days at 1 lesson per day; 33 days at 2 lessons per day

Corrective Reading B1

Enter: Sucessfully complete CR Level A or Place Level B1 on CR placement test

Exit: Successfully complete 65 lessons and demonstrate skills

Duration: 65 days at 1 lesson per day; 33 days at 2 lessons per day

Corrective Reading B2

Enter: Sucessfully complete CR Level B1 or Place Level B2 on CR placement test

Exit: Successfully complete 65 lessons and demonstrate skills

Duration: 65 days at 1 lesson per day; 33 days at 2 lessons per day

Corrective Reading C

Enter: Sucessfully complete CR Level B2 or Place Level C on CR placement test

Exit: Successfully complete 120 lessons

Duration: 120 days at 1 lesson per day; 60 days at 2 lessons per day

Language! C/D

Enter: 6th grade students or students that successfully complete CR C

Exit: Complete Language! C/D and demonstrate skills on external assessments

Duration: One year

Language! E/F

Enter: 7th grade students or students that successfully complete Language! C/D

Exit: Complete language! E/F and demonstrate skills on external assessments

Duration: One year

LA plus Read to Achieve N/C

Enter: 8th grade students or students that successfully complete Language! E/F

Exit: Complete LA and RTA N/C and demonstrate skills on external assessments

Duration: One year

23

effectiveness of the program or intervention. Failure to evaluate and address marginal or noneffective systems will result in an increased number of individual students requiring individual interventions. Such an approach is less efficient and difficult to sustain because schools will have many individual students to address. The concept of evaluating systems is revisited in Chapter 6.

Changing the Way Secondary Schools Do Business . . .

If secondary schools have a tiered support structure where students immediately receive intervention aligned to their instructional needs, they will go a long way toward improving student success and reducing many of the complications associated with poor achievement and failure (truancy, low motivation, behaviors, etc.). As important as a school's structure is to successful implementation of RTI, other considerations are also critical, including

- **Strong Instructional Leadership**—principals who are knowledgeable regarding instruction and interventions, who know effective school research, and ensure schools are organized accordingly
- **Implementation**—planning for and understanding the various stages of organizational change
- **Consensus and Commitment**—getting staff members to buy-in and support the program
- **Alignment of Initiatives**—taking stock of current initiatives; what needs to be continued, consolidated, or eliminated
- **Capacity Building**—increasing all the things necessary to get things done
- **Resources**—providing time, personnel, funding, and physical space
- **Fidelity**—doing things as prescribed

Each of the above priorities is examined in more depth starting with perhaps the single most important element—instructional leadership.

INSTRUCTIONAL LEADERSHIP FROM THE PRINCIPAL

The success of RTI schools is tied directly to the support and leadership provided by the administration. An instructional leader

- establishes clear instructional priorities for the school; for example, students with skill deficits will receive specific research

RTI Framework

RTI Framework
Problem Solving Systems and Individuals

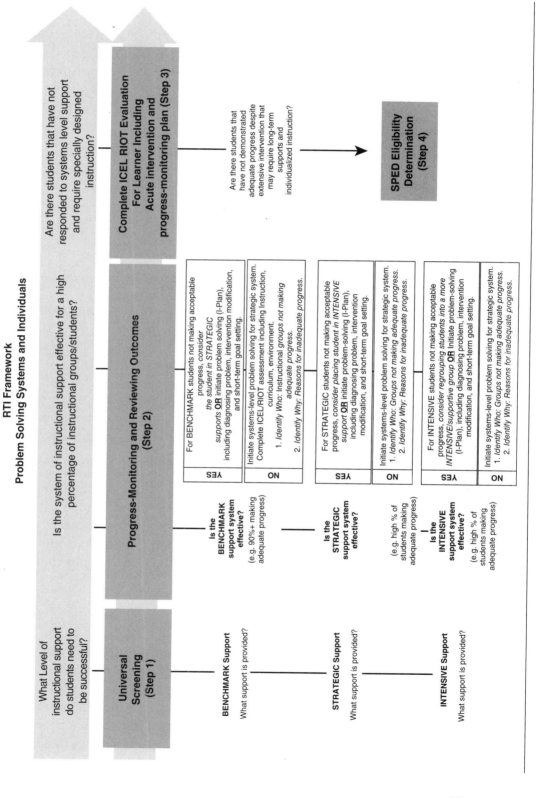

What Level of instructional support do students need to be successful?

Is the system of instructional support effective for a high percentage of instructional groups/students?

Are there students that have not responded to systems level support and require specially designed instruction?

Universal Screening (Step 1)

Progress-Monitoring and Reviewing Outcomes (Step 2)

Complete ICEL RIOT Evaluation For Learner Including Acute intervention and progress-monitoring plan (Step 3)

Are there students that have not demonstrated adequate progress despite extensive intervention that may require long-term supports and individualized instruction?

SPED Eligibility Determination (Step 4)

BENCHMARK Support
What support is provided?

Is the BENCHMARK support system effective?
(e.g. 90%+ making adequate progress)

YES	For BENCHMARK students not making acceptable progress, *consider the student in STRATEGIC supports* **OR** initiate problem solving (I-Plan), including diagnosing problem, intervention modification, and short-term goal setting.
NO	Initiate systems-level problem solving for strategic system. Complete ICEL/RIOT assessment including Instruction, curriculum, environment. 1. *Identify Who: Instructional groups not making adequate progress.* 2. *Identify Why: Reasons for inadequate progress.*

STRATEGIC Support
What support is provided?

Is the STRATEGIC support system effective?
(e.g. high % of students making adequate progress)

YES	For STRATEGIC students not making acceptable progress, *consider placing student in INTENSIVE support* **OR** initiate problem-solving (I-Plan), including diagnosing problem, intervention modification, and short-term goal setting.
NO	Initiate systems-level problem solving for strategic system. 1. *Identify Who: Groups not making adequate progress.* 2. *Identify Why: Reasons for inadequate progress.*

INTENSIVE Support
What support is provided?

Is the INTENSIVE support system effective?
(e.g. high % of students making adequate progress)

YES	For INTENSIVE students not making acceptable progress, *consider regrouping students into a more INTENSIVE/supportive group* **OR** Initiate problem-solving (I-Plan), including diagnosing problem, intervention modification, and short-term goal setting.
NO	Initiate systems-level problem solving for strategic system. 1. *Identify Who: Groups not making adequate progress.* 2. *Identify Why: Reasons for inadequate progress.*

validated interventions as part of their school day, or students failing one or more classes will be required to attend before and after school tutoring;

- has a "whatever it takes" attitude—does not allow circumstances, lack of resources, or resistance from staff derail the system;
- actively leads improvement—has a deep understanding of the goal and how to get there, holds others accountable but provides necessary supports;
- attends all staff trainings;
- attends or runs leadership team meetings—keeps everyone focused on goals and models expected behavior;
- assures that updates are on every staff meeting agenda;
- observes instruction in all classes—knows what to look for—provides combination of support and pressure;
- provides training and support for staff needing extra help learning research-based programs and interventions;
- does regular "walk-throughs" in intervention classrooms to assure interventions are being carried out as designed;
- attends or leads regularly scheduled RTI meetings—emphasizes focus on establishing and improving systems;
- attends or leads data meetings;
- brings in outside expertise and builds inside expertise;
- provides appropriate support and pressure to staff members; and
- organizes resources and school structure to maximize student performance.

Leadership that can manage complex change at the school level is a fundamental requirement for the successful implementation and sustainability of RTI. No silver bullets, quick fixes, interventions, or strategies will instantly provide better student results. Leadership must understand the magnitude, complexity, and commitment for the required systems change that will, over time, lead to improved outcomes.

Implementation

The implementation research of Fixsen, Naoom, Blasé, Friedman, and Wallace (2005) concludes that the organizational change process required to implement RTI can take two to four years. To achieve improved outcomes for students, both effective interventions and effective implementation must be present. Six stages of implementation have been identified. They are recursive, not linear or hierarchical stages. Unique factors in a school (i.e., high levels of staff turnover) can create the need to move to a previous stage. The stages of implementation as defined by Fixsen et al. (2005) are as follows:

1. Exploration: Identifying the need for change, learning about possible interventions that may be solutions, learning about what it takes to implement the innovation effectively, developing stakeholders and champions, deciding to proceed

2. Installation: Establishing the resources needed to use an innovation and resources required to implement the innovation with fidelity and good outcomes for students

3. Initial Implementation: The first use of intervention practices by newly trained teachers and others working in a school and district environment that is just learning how to support the new ways of teaching (sometimes referred to as *the awkward stage*)

4. Full Implementation: The skillful use of an innovation well-integrated into the repertoire of teachers and routinely supported by building and district administrators

5. Innovation: The advances in knowledge and skill that come from evaluated changes in how teachers and others make use of a science-based intervention

6. Sustainability: Persistent and skillful support for teachers and staff who are using an innovation effectively, with each cohort of teachers achieving better results than the last. This is sometimes referred to as *regeneration* defined as the set of procedures that allow a system to continually compare valued outcomes against current practice and modify practices to continue to achieve valued outcomes as the context changes over time.

Consensus and Commitment

If initiatives are implemented without establishing a shared commitment and consensus of staff, the school improvement process can become an attempt-attack-abandon cycle. A proactive leader recognizes that RTI is an adaptive and complex change process that challenges staff habits, beliefs, and values. Gaining consensus that the school's mission is to improve the learning outcomes for all students creates a willingness to examine practices in light of their impact on learning (Eaker, Dufour, & Dufour, 2002). RTI has been described as an approach for redesigning and establishing teaching and learning environments that are effective, efficient, relevant, and durable for all students, families, and educators. The focus shifts from "What's wrong with this child?" to "What positive and preventive supports can we provide to help this child be successful?". The RTI framework emphasizes that a problem is no longer within the student but an indication that the system is not responsive to the needs of all students.

An effective way to share the responsibility of consensus building and commitment to RTI is to establish a building leadership team. The team's membership should include the building administrator and staff with expertise in data analysis, content expertise, intervention expertise, behavior, and instructional coaching. A consideration for the composition of the team is approximately three-fourths of the members represent general education and one-fourth represents special education.

A good first step to implementation is to assess the degree to which the supports, infrastructure, and features of RTI already exist. An RTI Implementation Checklist is one way to obtain this baseline information. The implementation checklist also identifies the components that need to be established for a comprehensive and systems approach to RTI. Below is a copy of the checklist.

Alignment of Initiatives

Systems alignment is an essential ingredient for a continuous school improvement model. Several initiatives, frameworks, and models are often part of the schools' continuum of learning supports (e.g., RTI, PBIS, PLC, What Works in Schools [Marzano], accreditation models, etc.). Schools would benefit from completing a cross-walk analysis of current initiatives. The analyses should begin with a clear articulation of the school's vision, mission, and goals. Initiatives, frameworks, and building teams can be matched for purpose, alignment, or overlap to determine what needs to be continued, consolidated, or eliminated. RTI should be conceptualized as a coherent framework that integrates curriculum and assessment. Schools that develop a clear definition of RTI create shared ownership and common ground (Tackett, Roberts, Baker, & Scammaca, 2009).

Capacity Building

Capacity building is defined as increasing the competencies, resources, and motivation of individuals and groups of people to get important things done (Fullan & Quinn, 2010). A school culture that fosters relationships, collaboration, shared decision making, instructional coaching, mentoring, and ongoing professional development builds the capacity of

RTI Implementation Checklist—Secondary Schools

	Elements of a Schoolwide Approach	YES	NO	PARTIAL	Comments
1.	Arrange system to meet the needs of students, including those with reading and math skill deficits.				
	A. Are reading and math interventions available for students with skill deficits?				
	B. Strategic-level students receive targeted intervention to address specific areas of need.				
	C. Intensive students are placed in comprehensive interventions for one to two class periods per day, five days per week.				
	D. Is a sufficient number of staff allocated?				
	E. Has staff been assigned in a way such that necessary interventions can be delivered to the full range of students each day?				
2.	Use universal screening and functional assessment (e.g., phonics screening, etc.) to identify and place students according to instructional needs.				
	A. Screening assessments are administered to identify students with math and/or reading skill deficits.				
	B. Diagnostic assessments are used to identify specific instructional focus for Strategic level students.				
	C. Intensive-level students are administered placement tests.				
3.	Use differentiated instruction to meet the needs of instructional groups.				
	A. Are students grouped according to identified instructional focus area (homogenously by performance level/skill deficits)?				
	B. Are students grouped based on program recommendation?				
	C. Are group sizes appropriate to ensure student success in intervention?				
4.	Use research-based interventions and instructional practices.				
	A. All instructional reading/math programs and materials are research validated.				
	B. Instructional programs are aligned to student instructional needs.				
	C. Are intervention programs implemented with fidelity?				
	D. Are fidelity checks conducted regularly?				
5.	Conduct frequent progress monitoring to ensure adequate growth.				
	A. In-program assessment (i.e., end of unit tests, etc.) are administered as required?				
	B. Out-of-program assessments are administered (monthly for Strategic students and twice monthly for Intensive students).				
	C. Data are used for instructional decision making (i.e., to adjust instructional groups, evaluate effectiveness of instruction, etc.)				
	D. Data meetings have been established and occur regularly.				

	Elements of a Schoolwide Approach	YES	NO	PARTIAL	Comments
6.	Provide ongoing professional development to support system-wide structures of instruction.				
	A. Is training provided for teachers (i.e., staff receives adequate training prior to teaching programs)?				
	B. Are program specific consultants brought in to observe in classrooms and provide ongoing support and training?				
	C. Are in-service sessions developed around implementation issues identified by the building/district administrators?				
	D. Do building administrators conduct classroom walk-throughs during intervention?				
	E. Are new teachers provided the necessary program training?				
7.	Use data to evaluate effectiveness of schoolwide system.				
	A. Does the school have a method to evaluate effectiveness of instructional supports/systems (i.e., Benchmark, Strategic, and Intensive)?				
	B. Less effective systems are identified and addressed (improved).				
	C. A schoolwide team is established to evaluate the effectiveness of systems.				
8.	Use problem-solving teams to identify and address unhealthy systems.				
	A. Building-level teams identify systems in need of support and are skilled at identifying actions to improve systems.				
	B. Action plans are created to address improve systems.				
	C. Outcome goals and evaluation methods are identified to evaluate the effectiveness of action plans.				
9.	Develop intervention plans for students whose needs cannot be adequately addressed within the system (e.g., require intervention/instruction not available as part of the overall system).				
	A. Intervention plans are created using a formal problem-solving process.				
	B. Goals of student intervention plans are clearly specified and regularly monitored.				
	C. Students in need of intervention are first addressed at the system level before being referred to the building level team.				
	D. Student level teams exist for the purpose of improving student performance rather than for referral.				
10.	Use information relevant to a student's response to intervention (progress-monitoring data, review of intervention duration, intensity, and fidelity) as part of process for determining eligibility for special education.				
	A. Students considered for special education have received intervention within effective systems.				
	B. Students considered for special education have received research-validated interventions aligned to their instructional needs and for an extended period of time.				
	C. Progress-monitoring information, history of interventions, and results are used in determining eligibility for special education.				

the instructional staff and the school to improve student outcomes. Ample evidence exists that "one-shot" in-services and professional development trainings rarely improve skills and practices of teachers.

Systems, resources, and competence are needed to maintain effects, support high fidelity of implementation, expand applications, and sustain implementation (Sugai, 2007).

Resources

The implementation of RTI requires "a different way of doing business" (Batsche, 2006). RTI cannot be viewed as an add-on or afterthought. The successful implementation of RTI requires an examination of current practices and a reallocation of resources, including

- Scheduling time for universal screening, progress monitoring, professional development, team meetings, core instruction, interventions, and so on
- Staff instructional duties
- Funding sources
- Physical space for instruction

Fidelity

Fidelity refers to all aspects of RTI (intervention, assessment, tiers, etc.) *Fidelity of implementation* is defined as "the delivery of content and instructional strategies in the way in which they were designed and intended to be delivered accurately and consistently" (National Center on Response to Intervention, 2012). Assuring fidelity is not as simple as completing a checklist or an observation of instruction. Fidelity is an integral part of every feature of RTI rather than a separate component. Schools need to self-assess at the surface (climate) level of the system (i.e., vision, mission, goals, infrastructure, etc.) and at a deeper (culture) level (i.e., values, beliefs, norms, leadership, etc.). Schools also need to assess instructional and assessment fidelity at the classroom level to ensure adherence to the research-based design of the intervention and assessment.

At the school level, RTI implementation with fidelity means ensuring the following are in place:

- An assessment system that provides information about students' risk status
- An assessment system that provides information about students' progress during instruction

- Curriculum, interventions, and strategies that are evidence based
- A horizontal and vertical alignment across tiers and grade levels
- Clear communication and feedback with staff about goals, roles, and responsibilities
- Fidelity checks that are routinely scheduled and analyzed with staff to improve implementation and instruction
- Practices that are aligned and integrated to promote sustainability
- Policies, procedures, practices, and a common vocabulary that are agreed-upon and documented (National Center on Response to Intervention, 2012)

CONCLUSION

Systems change for secondary schools is complex and challenging. In short, systems resist change, and as a result, the successful transformations must be well planned out. A systems approach to RTI uses protocols where instructional supports are defined and preestablished. Students are provided supports according to need, and assessments are used to inform decision making. Additional yet critical considerations to redesign secondary systems include instructional leadership, implementation planning, consensus and commitment, aligning initiatives, capacity building, and resources.

Blank worksheets and user forms discussed in this section are available for download at **www.partnersforlearning.org**.

Teaching and Learning in Secondary Schools

3

OBJECTIVES:

- Understand key considerations to improving core instruction
- Understand the distinction between supports and interventions
- Know the curriculum formats that cause problems for struggling learners
- Know how Good Standing could be used to improve student motivation
- Understand why interventions must be research based and/or validated
- Know the difference between Tier 2 and Tier 3 interventions
- Be able to explain what additional considerations beyond specific interventions are important

---

Reading difficulties are common throughout the United States. In schools that serve minority populations and those students living in poverty, the problem is even more prevalent. Research shows that students do not "outgrow" reading problems (Francis, Shaywitz, Stuebing, Shaywitz, & Fletcher, 1996) and can be prevented when students in the primary grades are provided with quality classroom reading instruction along with additional small-group intervention when needed (Mathes & Denton, 2002). Remediating serious reading difficulties for older students is difficult but achievable. Quality reading instruction is *powerful*. Brain imaging research has demonstrated that the way the brain processes information is different in typically developing readers than in those at risk for or experiencing reading difficulties, but that these processing patterns in the brains of struggling readers—even those with severe dyslexia—can actually change in a period of a few weeks when they are provided with concentrated, powerful reading instruction (see, for example, Denton, Fletcher, Simos, Papanicolaou, & Anthony, 2007).

This chapter explores ways to improve teaching and learning in secondary schools, focusing on ways to improve content area learning as well as keys to effectively addressing students with specific skill deficits through research-validated interventions. Specific strategies are presented for improving the effectiveness of content/core instruction including (1) making instruction more engaging and active for students, (2) making instruction more explicit and systematic, (3) developing a plan for vocabulary instruction that is systematic, and (4) differentiated instruction. Tier 1, 2, and 3 interventions are defined and explored. Specific intervention programs are presented along with important considerations for maximizing outcomes when using such interventions.

IMPROVING CONTENT AREA INSTRUCTION FOR SECONDARY STUDENTS

As schools adopt and implement programs and approaches that are supported by scientific research, it is important that teachers understand what makes good instruction and receive the professional development and support they need. The professional development should be aligned to what research supports regarding effective instructional practices.

Despite a lot of information on how to make instruction more effective, everyday core instruction too often employs formats problematic for diverse learners and struggling students, including

- Overly student directed/generative
- Spiral curriculum
- Limited consideration of prior knowledge
- Lack of explicit instruction targeting critical concepts and skills
- Limited scaffolding
- Too little guided practice and too much independent practice—resulting in wrong practice that is difficult to correct later
- Limited opportunities to apply and generalize newly acquired skills

When considering the characteristics of struggling learners (e.g., memory problems, poor organizational skills, attention difficulties, etc.), it is not surprising poor teaching methodologies are often responsible for poor academic outcomes/lack of student achievement. The percentage of struggling students could be greatly reduced if more effective instructional practices were utilized across all classrooms in middle and high schools.

"What does powerful classroom instruction look like? Research-supported characteristics of quality classroom instruction can be summarized as follows:

1. Teach essential skills and strategies.

2. Provide differentiated instruction based on assessment results and adapt instruction to meet students' needs.

3. Provide explicit and systematic instruction with lots of practice. During acquisition, closely monitor student performance and provide immediate and specific feedback. Practice should be cumulative over time.

4. Provide opportunities to apply skills and strategies in reading and writing meaningful text with teacher support.

5. Don't just 'cover' critical content; be sure students learn it by teaching to mastery—monitor student progress regularly and reteach as necessary." (Denton, n.d.)

KEYS TO IMPROVING TIER I/CONTENT AREA INSTRUCTION: TIER I CORE INSTRUCTION

At the secondary school level, Tier I are the content area classes designed to cover grade-level standards. Such instruction is designed to

- Benefit the majority of students
- Enable the majority of students to meet academic and behavioral expectations
- Prepare students for postsecondary life and college

Although a Benchmark/Tier I student is low risk for academic failure, the effectiveness of core instruction plays a critical role in student learning outcomes and whether students pass or fail. Content instruction is not intended to provide specialized intervention to address specific skill deficits. It should, and can, however, incorporate effective practices designed to support and maximize diverse student learning. Listed below are potential "fixes" to ensure core instruction is aligned to the research on effective instructional practices as well as important information on how the brain learns (and retains) information.

FIX IT #1—Maximize the use of the instructional strategies

McREL's Nine Categories of Instructional Strategies

Category	Definition
Setting Objectives and Providing Feedback	Provide students with a direction for learning and with information about how well they are performing relative to a particular learning objective so they can improve their performance.
Reinforcing Effort and Providing Recognition	Enhance students' understanding of the relationship between effort and achievement by addressing students' attitudes and beliefs about learning. Provide students with abstract tokens of recognition or praise for their accomplishments related to the attainment of a goal.
Cooperative Learning	Provide students with opportunities to interact with one another in ways that enhance their learning.
Cues, Questions, and Advance Organizers	Enhance students' ability to retrieve, use, and organize what they already know about a topic.
Nonlinguistic Representations	Enhance students' ability to represent and elaborate on knowledge using mental images.
Summarizing and Note Taking	Enhance students' ability to synthesize information and organize it in a way that captures the main ideas and supporting details.
Assigning Homework and Providing Practice	Extend the learning opportunities for students to practice, review, and apply knowledge. Enhance students' ability to reach the expected level of proficiency for a skill or process.

Category	Definition
Identifying Similarities and Differences	Enhance students' understanding of and ability to use knowledge by engaging them in mental processes that involve identifying ways in which items are alike and different.
Generating and Testing Hypotheses	Enhance students' understanding of and ability to use knowledge by engaging them in mental processes that involve making and testing hypotheses.

Source: Adapted from Pitler et al., 2012. Used with permission.

FIX IT #2—Increase Student Engagement

Active learning involves providing opportunities for students to meaningfully talk and listen, write, read, and reflect on the content, ideas, issues, and concerns of an academic subject (Meyers & Jones, 1993).

There are several types of active engagement:

- Group oral responses
- Paired partner responses
- Individual oral responses
- Written responses
- Physical responses (Archer, 2007)

High levels of active engagement during lessons are associated with higher levels of achievements and student motivation (Ryan & Deci, 2000). Active engagement is a key feature of well-delivered explicit and systematic instruction.

Instructional strategies that increase engagement:

- Explicit instruction
- Increased opportunities for response (choral, partner, written, individual)
- Peer-assisted learning
- Structured thinking and partner rehearsal

Provided is an Active Participation Template. It outlines specific steps to make core instruction more explicit and engaging. Each step of the template is paired with examples to illustrate the exact wording that could be used when utilizing the instructional routines.

Purpose: Increase student responses and engagement during all phases of instruction.

		EXAMPLE
INTRODUCTION **TEACHING STRATEGY: FOCUS** and **THINK TIME**	**Engage students when introducing topics or explaining directions.** A. Students look at teacher, board or point at key words in book during introduction. B. State topic. Students repeat. C. Teacher presents key information. Students explain key aspects to partners. D. Script think time – given	A. "Look/point to (title/paragraph/word) on p.___" B. "Today we are reviewing the central nervous system" "What is our topic?" (choral response) C. Teacher presents key information. "Partners, briefly discuss what you remember about the central nervous system" D. Ask question. Pause 3-5 seconds. "What's the answer? " (Signal).
RESPONSES **TEACHING STRATEGY: SIGNALS**	**Students actively engaged/respond during all phases of instruction.** A. Students respond chorally when responses require short responses, or B. Students respond to a partner during expanded responses.	A. "As you will recall, there are sensory nerves and motor nerves. <u>Sensory nerves carry messages to the brain and motor nerves carry messages from the brain.</u> Everybody, sensory nerves carry messages where? (choral response). Everybody, motor nerves carry messages where? (choral response) B. "Partner A, explain to Partner B what sensory nerves do, Partner B listen for accuracy" "Partner B, explain to Partner A what motor nerves do, Partner B listen for accuracy"
MASTERY TEACHING **TEACHING STRATEGY: INDIVIDUAL TURNS** and **CORRECTION PROCEDURE**	**A. Students are called on for individual responses.** Call on students in an unpredictable order with student name last. ✓ Ensure students understand ✓ Opportunity to check mastery of students who may struggle ✓ Sends message all students must be engaged and ready to respond at all times B. Inaccurate responses are immediately corrected using "My turn" or "It is…" format. Follow all errors with a delayed test before ending the lesson.	A. Group then individual response: 1. "I'll name different messages, you tell me if each message goes **to** the brain or **from** the brain – your foot hurts. Everybody…" (Choral response) 2. "So is it a sensory nerve or a motor nerve? Everybody…" 3. Repeat for several examples. 4. "Individual turns. Be ready for me to call on you. Your stomach hurts. Is it a sensory nerve or motor nerve? Maria?" B. Group or individual student responds incorrectly: "My turn. If your stomach hurts the message goes **to** the brain. It is a sensory nerve. Everybody, what kind of nerve is it if your stomach hurts?" (Choral response)
EXPANDED RESPONSES **TEACHING STRATEGY: VERIFICATION** and **EXTENSION**	**A. Check Students' Understanding** Option 1: Deep processing questions Option 2: Examples/Non-examples Option 3: Students generate examples Option 4: Sentence starter B. **Verification:** Each time the group or an individual student states an answer, repeat the answer back to them.	A. Questions: 1. "What could interfere with sensory nerve messages?" 2. "Would feeling pain be an example of a motor nerve?" 3. "Tell your partner an example of a motor nerve." 4. "Explain to your partner what sensory nerves do." 5. Start your sentence by saying, 'Motor nerves….' **Then** tell why." B. Yes. Motor nerves carry messages from the brain.

FIX IT #3—Make Instruction More Explicit and Systematic

Explicit instruction . . . does not leave anything to chance, and does not make assumptions about skills and knowledge that children acquire on their own.

—Torgesen, 2004

Academic failure can often be attributed to the erroneous assumption that all students know how to complete a task without explicit lessons. More than any other factor, explicit instruction is essential to student achievement. Research supports that skills, processes, strategies, and content must be explicitly and systematically taught. They must be modeled and practiced in multiple settings with a variety of materials. A gradual withdrawal of teacher support must follow until the student achieves the desired level of automaticity and is independent. Outstanding and effective teachers understand the following sequential components of explicit instruction:

- **Direct Explanation** tells why the skill or strategy is important and when it is used (e.g., the teacher names and defines the skill, process, content, or strategy to be learned).
- **Teacher Modeling** overtly demonstrates a skill, process, content, or strategy. Modeling provides concrete examples for students and a greater likelihood for mastery.
- **Guided Practice** allows students to practice the skill or strategy independently or in small groups, prompts, specific corrective feedback, and praise are provided. Teacher support gradually fades as the student takes responsibility for using the skill, process, or strategy independently.
- **Independent Practice** provides students with multiple opportunities to apply the newly acquired skill, process, content, or strategy on their own. Students can continue to review and practice as necessary.
- **Formative Assessment** evaluates the mastery of the new skill, process, content, or strategy. It allows the teacher to design future instruction to target skills, process, content, and strategies that in turn require additional review and instruction.

FIX IT #4—Use Explicit Vocabulary Instruction

As mentioned in the introduction, more than 60 percent of middle and high school students scored below proficient in reading. Federal studies suggest students' reading performance may not improve until they have a better grasp of vocabulary. In fact, nationwide vocabulary skills closely track reading comprehension. The top 25 percent of readers turned in an average 225 point vocabulary score on a 500 point scale; the weakest 25 percent scored only 177 points (U.S. Department of Education, 2010).

Although the correlation between vocabulary and reading comprehension, and in fact, between vocabulary and academic success, is well established, reviews of education statistics reveal performances are not improving over time. For example, fourth and eighth graders' vocabulary scores were unchanged from 2009 to 2011; a trend as true of the past as it is today.

How do secondary students get so far behind despite years of vocabulary exposure and instruction? Research points to the fact that students with vocabulary deficits were behind entering kindergarten (students often enter with half the language skills as their vocabulary-rich peers). According to Sharon Darling, President of the National Center for Family Literacy, schools are not helping narrow the gap. Students who enter at a disadvantage stay at a disadvantage as they move through school. In other words, students who were in trouble early stay in the same degree of academic trouble as they move through school. Robert Pondiscio (2012), of the Core Knowledge Foundation, wrote, "Demographics isn't destiny but vocabulary might be. . . . Vocabulary is the skill of skills."

How to Help Build Students' Vocabularies

Ways of building vocabulary can be classified into two categories: (1) exposure opportunities and (2) direct teaching. *Exposure* simply means giving students lots of meaningful learning opportunities that include vocabulary. *Direct teaching*, on the other hand, means directly teaching the words students need to know. Examples of each include

Exposure to vocabulary

- Encourage and assign wide reading
  - Reading best suited for proficient readers
  - Wide level reading (simple and challenging)
  - One or more hours per day

- Expose students to high quality oral language
  - Use rich vocabulary in and out of classroom settings
  - Use of vocabulary-rich technologies

- Promoting word consciousness
  - Knowledge and interest in words
  - Activities with words—learning centers, word games, partner work

- Teaching independent word-learning strategies
  - Efficient use of dictionaries (consider using student-friendly dictionaries)
  - The use of word parts (prefixes, suffixes, roots, compounds)
  - The use of context clues

Direct Teaching

- Provide explicit instruction of specific word knowledge
  - Teach both academic and high utility words
  - Use both definitional and contextual information about word meanings
  - Involve students actively in word learning
  - Use discussion to teach the meaning of new words and to provide meaningful information about the words

Explicit Vocabulary Instruction: A Closer Look

Whereas schools can and should identify ways to expand and maximize students' exposure to high quality oral language, the focus of this discussion is on how to directly teach content specific/academic words.

The research basis for using explicit instruction to teach vocabulary is impressive (Baker, Simmons, & Kameenui, 1995; Beck, McKeown, & Kucan, 2002; Biemiller, 2004; Hall, n.d.; Feldman & Kinsella, 2005; Graves, 2000; Marzano, 2004; Rosenshine & Stevens, 1986; Stahl & Fairbanks, 1986). Directly and explicitly teaching vocabulary is one of the most efficient ways to introduce new vocabulary. In isolation or in single classroom teaching, vocabulary will have less of an impact than if vocabulary is taught across all academic settings.

A Schoolwide Vocabulary Plan

A schoolwide vocabulary plan can have a powerful effect on improving student word knowledge if implemented thoughtfully, across settings, and for extended periods of time. Single shots of vocabulary instruction are likely to never deliver words into long-term memory. Brain research provides insight regarding how to maximize the conditions necessary to make memory more reliable, including memory of words. In short, repetition is key. Most information disappears from memory within minutes; those that survive the fragile first learning will strengthen with time and practice. The best way to get vocabulary into long-term memory is to incorporate words in context gradually in a clear and concise fashion and then repeat them in time intervals, ensuring perfect practice along the way. Explicit instruction can help reduce confusion and wrong practice when learning new vocabulary. The use of explicit instruction is aligned with brain research. Below is an outline for a systematic schoolwide vocabulary plan that incorporates explicit instruction and routines as well as meaningful and varied practice activities distributed across time. Suggestions for screening for vocabulary deficits and systematic interventions are also provided.

USING BRAIN RESEARCH TO IMPROVE INSTRUCTIONAL PRACTICES

CONDITIONS NECESSARY FOR PRACTICE TO IMPROVE PERFORMANCE

1. The learner must be sufficiently motivated to improve performance.

2. The learner must have all the knowledge necessary to understand the different ways the new knowledge or skill can be applied.

3. The learner must understand how to apply the knowledge to deal with a particular situation.

4. The learner must be able to analyze the result of that application and know what needs to be changed to improve performance in the future.

THE TEACHER'S ROLE

1. Select the smallest amount of material that will have the maximum meaning for the learner.

2. Model the application process step-by-step. Studies repeatedly show the brain uses observation as a means for determining the spatial learning needed to master a motor skill (Petrosini et al., 2003).

3. Insist the practice occur in the teacher's presence over a short period of time while the student is focused on the learning.

4. Watch the practice and provide the student with prompt and specific feedback.

Vocabulary Plan: Step 1: Systematic Screening and Intervention

Of course, the best plan is to intervene early and prevent long-term complications associated with poor vocabulary skills. At the secondary level, however, schools can still provide meaningful intervention for students with severe deficiencies. Vocabulary intervention for older students is designed to improve student learning in content classes by filling in missing basic vocabulary often referred to as *Tier 2 words* (high utility words that appear frequently in everyday settings). Typically, students below the 10th percentile on valid vocabulary assessments are considered significantly impacted and are candidates for intervention.

INTERVENTIONS FOR STUDENTS WITH SEVERE VOCABULARY DEFICITS

- Reasoning and Writing SRA
- Corrective Reading Comprehension SRA
- Language for Writing SRA

PROGRAMS FOR ENGLISH LANGUAGE LEARNERS

- Academic Vocabulary for English Learners (Grades 4–12)–Voyager Sopris Learning
- Direct Instruction Spoken English (Grades 4–12)–Voyager Sopris Learning

---

Vocabulary Plan: Step Two: Teaching Content/Academic Vocabulary

The plan presented below can be applied to any academic area in which learning vocabulary is important, including language arts, science, math, social studies, computers, trade professions, and so on. The steps outlined allow academic vocabulary to be explicitly taught and practiced during specific content area instruction. The steps include

1. Identify and teach key academic/Common Core vocabulary words.

2. Use student-friendly definitions.

3. Create concrete visual representation for each word, including the word definition and picture.

4. Use weekly instructional routines for introducing words.

5. Teach vocabulary in context where it appears in the curriculum.

6. Establish extensive opportunities for students to practice and use vocabulary in a variety of contexts but differentiated to ensure meaningful, correct practice.

7. Assess for mastery, reteach as necessary.

8. Establish progress-monitoring assessments to ensure vocabulary words are retained in long-term memory and generalized to settings beyond the classroom.

Carrying Out Systematic Vocabulary Instruction

Provided is a systematic approach to teaching academic vocabulary, in context, incorporating the above eight steps. A five-day instructional routine is followed, including

Day 1 and 2 (Monday and Tuesday)

Key academic words are introduced during the first ten minutes of each class (words for the week) for two consecutive days—typically Monday and Tuesday. Think of this as a "bell ringer activity." Students are told these are critical words/key vocabulary that will appear during the week's content. A teaching template can be used outlining the specific steps to be followed when introducing new words. An example template is provided on p. 45. The use of such a template guides teachers instructional practices—ensuring words are directly taught, students are actively engaged/responding, student-friendly definitions are provided, a visual representation of the word is paired with the definition, and opportunities for guided practice are provided prior to students completing independent activities/practice.

Weekly words are chosen from a prioritized list of key academic words, aligned to the Common Core or other State Standards, and embedded into the curriculum.

To teach the Common Core ELA words in seventh grade, for instance, a total of 230 key words would need to be covered during the course of the school year (for most school terms an average of 6.4 words per week would need to be taught). Presented on p. 46 are the number of Common Core words we have identified by grade level for both ELA and mathematics.

Instructional Routine for Teaching Critical Unknown Vocabulary Words

INSTRUCTIONAL ROUTINE FOR TEACHING CRITICAL, UNKNOWN VOCABULARY WORDS		
PROCEDURES: Use to introduce and review NEW Vocabulary words		Ⓥ
STEP 1	**Introduce the Word** **A.** Write the word on board. **B.** Read word. Students repeat. **C.** Repeat for unfamiliar words.	**EXAMPLE** "This word is *correlation*." "What word?"
STEP 2	**Present a Student-Friendly Definition** **A.** Tell students explanation, or **B.** Have students read explanation with you.	"*Correlation* is the degree which two variables are related." "What is correlation?
STEP 3	**Illustrate the Word with Examples** • Concrete examples • Visual representations • Verbal examples	"If you are looking how things are correlated – you are determining their relationship." "Good health has been found to be positively correlated to daily exercise."
STEP 4	**Check Students' Understanding** Option 1: Deep processing questions Option 2: Examples/Non-Examples Option 3: Students generate examples Option 4: Sentence starter	"Do you think exposure to the sun would have any correlation to skin cancer?" "What would you not expect to be correlated?" "Tell your partner something a dirty car might be *correlated* to." "Give your partner a specific example of a correlation between two variables." "Start a sentence by saying, 'A good paying job might be correlated to . . .' Then tell why."

INSTRUCTIONAL ROUTINE FOR TEACHING CRITICAL, UNKNOWN VOCABULARY WORDS		
PROCEDURES: Use to introduce and review NEW Vocabulary words.		Ⓥ
STEP 1	**Introduce the Word** **D.** Write the word on board. **E.** Read word. Students repeat. **F.** Repeat for unfamiliar words.	**PROMPT** "This word is _____." (choral response) "What word?" (choral response)
STEP 2	**Present a Student-Friendly Definition** **C.** Tell students explanation, or **D.** Have students read explanation with you.	"The definition of _____ is _____" "What is _____?" (choral response)
STEP 3	**Illustrate the Word with Examples** • Concrete examples • Visual representations • Verbal examples	Illustrate the word with a concrete example (i.e., PowerPoint Slide). Give one or more clear examples of the word. Use the "I do, We do, You do" format.
STEP 4	**Check Students' Understanding** Option 1: Deep processing questions Option 2: Examples/Non-Examples Option 3: Students generate examples Option 4: Sentence starter	Use the following options as a means to ensure students fully understand the newly introduced vocabulary word. Use choral response, random individual turns, and partner practice to evaluate student understanding. Correct errors and misconceptions immediately (prevent wrong practice).
Western Regional Reading First Technical Assistance Center		

eSlide Sample

Reading/Language Arts Vocabulary—Grade 8

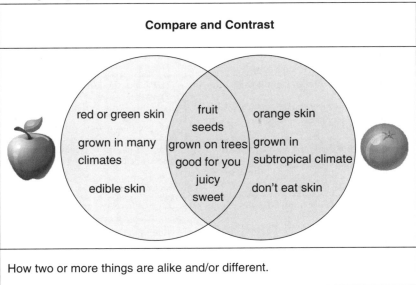

ELA			
WORDS	Academic	Common Core	Total Words
Grade K	5	217	222
Grade 1	24	166	190
Grade 2	39	212	251
Grade 3	91	217	308
Grade 4	77	244	321
Grade 5	83	212	295
Grade 6	101	178	279
Grade 7	46	230	276
Grade 8	61	221	282
Grade 9–10	75	199	274
Grade 11–12	60	208	268
Total K-12	662	2304	2966

Math			
WORDS	Academic	Common Core	Total Words
Grade K	39	88	127
Grade 1	67	72	139
Grade 2	81	90	171
Grade 3	191	95	286
Grade 4	204	108	312
Grade 5	202	106	308
Grade 6	86	110	196
Grade 7	124	106	230
Grade 8	116	91	207
Grade 9–12	121	220	341
Total K-12	1231	1086	2371

A complete list of academic and Common Core vocabulary words and student-friendly definitions by grade is available for download at www .partnersforlearning.org. For each Common Core vocabulary word the corresponding Common Core Standards are identified.

For the remainder of the week (Wednesday, Thursday, and Friday), teachers would have students engage in meaningful practice opportunities. Again, ten minutes per day at the beginning of each class can provide significant opportunities for students to engage in the academic vocabulary in meaningful ways. Consider developing practice activities that can be differentiated. Centers or work stations are an excellent form for differentiating practice. For practice opportunities, students enter the room and proceed directly to assigned stations where vocabulary tasks are prearranged. Five-minute rotations at each station will allow students to work at multiple stations and have an array of practice activities over the course of the week. Rotations also allow the opportunity for the teacher to provide direct instruction and guided practice to small groups of students. Centers and/or stations are a terrific way to differentiate instruction and practice because not all students will progress and master vocabulary at the same rate. Students' ability to practice using words will vary as well—some students will be ready for more sophisticated practice sooner than others.

The following templates provide suggestions for possible practice routines that can be incorporated for vocabulary practice.

Suggested Resources for Creating Meaningful
Vocabulary Practice Activities

Partners for Learning: Visual Vocabulary e-Slides and Common Core Vocabulary list (K–12): www.partnersforlearning.org

Florida Center for Reading Research: Vocabulary center activities for Grades K–5: http://www.fcrr.org/

Tennessee Department of Education: Vocabulary Activites: www.jc-schools.net/tutorials/vocab/

Quizlet: Create your own study materials: http://quizlet.com/

Vocabulary resource list: http://esu4vocabularystrategies.wikispaces .com/Vocabulary+Sites

Flocabulary (pairs rap with vocabulary): http://flocabulary.com/ subjects/

Jeopardy Labs: Create your own Jeopardy game at: https://jeopardy labs.com/

Instructional Strategies for Practicing Vocabulary Words Examples

INSTRUCTIONAL STRATEGIES FOR PRACTICING VOCABULARY WORDS EXAMPLE 1

Procedures: Consider using Bloom's Taxonomy as a means to give students meaningful interactions with the words

	Examples
1. Knowledge/Remember	The word correlation means? A. The answer to a division problem B. The relationship between two variables C. The study of numbers D. An object with four sides and four angles
2. Comprehension/Understand	Which word does not belong? _____ Why? _____ correlation perimeter relationship linked association
3. Application/Apply	Identify an outcome that would likely be correlated with each word. 1. unemployment: _____ 2. an unattended candle: _____ 3. prolonged exposure to the sun: _____ 4. hunger: _____
4. Analysis/Analyze	Analyze the following statements. Identify whether or not they are likely to be true. 1. A car's age is positively correlated to the likelihood it will breakdown. Explain? 2. A student that does not study is positively correlated to a high grade point average. Explain?

INSTRUCTIONAL STRATEGIES FOR PRACTICING VOCABULARY WORDS EXAMPLE 2

Procedures: Use the following activities for students to meaningfully engage/practice vocabulary words.

1. Yes/No/Why

EXAMPLES

Would you use **tons** to measure a mile?   Why?

Do **whole numbers** contain decimals?   Why?

2. Completion Activity

Name a **nonfiction** book _____.

A word that has an opposite meaning of another word is called an _____.

3. Graphic Organizer depicting relationship between vocabulary words

	Same	Opposite	Go Together	No Relation
analyze - data			X	
analyze - examine	X			
analyze - shell				X

Have students explain why they marked each box.

4. Word Lines

How surprised would you be if . . .

. . . you had a **flashback** to the day you were born?

. . . you read a **chapter** in 30 minutes?

Least Surprised. . . . .**Most Surprised**

5. Sentence Substitution

It is Joe's **opinion** that the movie was the best he's seen all year.

It is Joe's **personal judgment** that the movie was the best he's seen all year.

6. Meaningful Sentence Writing

Students write a sentence answering who, what, when, where, why, how questions.

*During the past week, name a situation in which you had a **conflict**? Why would a teacher **critique** a story written by a student?*

CORE (Consortium on Reading Excellence): Vocabulary Handbook: http://www.corelearn.com/

Motivation Math-Vocabulary Adventure: http://www.mentoring minds.com/products/subjects/vocabulary/vocabulary-adventure/vocabulary-adventure-student-edition.html

Finally, progress monitoring can be used to ensure students do not forget previously taught words. Vocabulary monitoring can be completed in two ways: (1) evaluating student mastery of vocabulary on a weekly basis in the form of mastery tests and (2) periodic progress monitoring to ensure words are retained in long-term memory. For the latter, consider using vocabulary monitoring assessments such as the examples provided below. Such monitoring is based on a sampling technique where words for the entire year are randomly assigned to probes, ten words to a probe. Students are administered the probes once a month. Each word has an equal chance of appearing on a probe as any other word. Thus, early in the year when most words have not been covered in the curriculum, students are not expected to score a high percentage correct. Through the year, however, as more words are taught, students' performance on the probes should incrementally improve. An aimline starting from 0 and progressing to 100 percent (from beginning of semester to the end of the semester) should be created with student performance closely tracking the progression from month to month. See example:

Eighth-Grade Progress-Monitoring TEST 1

Match the word with its definition by writing the correct number in the space provided.

2	effective	1	A part or feature of something
4	disadvantages	2	Identifies the result of a cause
8	central idea	3	An opinion that you form after thinking about many things; also means an ending or result
5	director	4	A condition or situation that makes it more difficult to succeed
6	simile	5	A person who guides the actors and directs the performance of the script for a play or movie

7	idiom	6	A figure of speech comparing two things using like or as
1	aspect	7	A phrase or expression in which the meaning is different than the literal meaning of the words
9	political	8	The main thought or focus of a work of literature
10	domain-specific words	9	Having to do with the study or practice of politics, politicians, or government
3	conclude/conclusion	10	Words that fall within a certain subject

Note: Vocabulary progress-monitoring measures aligned to the CCSS (such as the above example) are available at www.partnersforlearning.org.

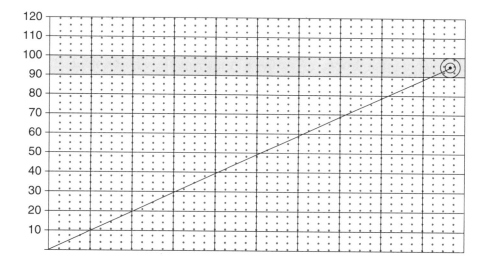

FIX IT #5—Differentiated Instruction

Differentiated Instruction is teaching with student variance in mind. It means starting where the kids are rather than adopting a standardized approach to teaching that seems to presume that all learners of a given age or grade are essentially alike. Thus, differentiated instruction is "responsive" teaching rather than "one-size-fits-all" teaching. It is critically important that content classes use differentiation extensively since students in such classes can vary widely in skills, vocabulary, and background knowledge.

Differentiated instruction is essential to meet the needs of all learners and necessitates thoughtful planning of instructional tasks. The release rate from teacher knowledge to student practice will be more gradual for some students than for others. Students may require a substantial amount of guided practice while others can progress quickly to independent practice. The variables of instruction such as frequency of instruction, opportunities for response, grouping, pacing, and amount of monitoring should be differentiated as well. Classroom teachers must be clear about what they are trying to teach and have concrete ways of evaluating student learning. Assessments are essential tools for informing differentiation.

Examples of differentiated instruction include

- **Flexible Grouping** is used to narrow the instructional range of a group of students. Groups are initially identified through universal screening and refined further as a result of data from diagnostic assessments and progress monitoring. Creating skill groups is an example of grouping that increases a school's capacity to meet the needs of all students.
- **Accommodations** are provided to allow students to gain access to content and/or complete tasks by altering the environment, changing the instructional format, or providing technology. Since accommodations do not alter the content that is taught, the expectation is that students will master grade-level skills.

  Examples of accommodations:
  o Alternate textbooks
  o Computer use
  o Appropriate reading level

Accommodations should not be confused with *modifications.* An accommodation is a change in the way student demonstrates mastery (e.g., orally vs. written). A modification is a change in what the student is expected to master (e.g., grade-level content). An accommodation provides access to knowledge and skills, but the student is still expected to master grade-level standards.

Before exploring specific interventions for students with academic skill deficits, it is important for secondary schools to consider what is in place to support all students across all classrooms regardless if students have specific skill deficits.

Example High School Reading Placement Pathway Plan

New students and those below 40th percentile on MAP receive AIMSweb (R-CBM & Maze)

Screening	Tier III INTENSIVE Below 10th Percentile on AIMS	Tier II STRATEGIC 11th–30th Percentile on the R-CBM and/or Maze			Tier I BENCHMARK 31st–70th Percentile 41% - 70%ile	Tier I ADVANCED 71st–99th Percentile
Grade-Level Assessments						
Diagnosis: Criteria	At or Below 10th percentile on R-CBM and or Maze	Strategic level reading skills (11th–30th percentile) Fusion placement test			MAP; R-CBM. Maze and/or Easy CBM Fast & Right	MAP, R-CBM. Maze and/or Easy CBM Demonstrates the need for additional challenge and advancement Fast & Right
Focus	COMPREHENSIVE	PHONICS	FLUENCY	COMPREHENSION	CORE CONTENT	ENRICHMENTS
Focus Skills	Basic reading skills: Letter/sound correspondence, decoding, fluency, vocabulary, comprehension	Targeted decoding skills	Automatically decoding words, reading high frequency, and phrasing sentences	Comprehension Skills and/or Strategies	Core coursework	Advanced Content Focus Comprehension Strategies Writing
Intervention	Core Replacement: CORRECTIVE READING Decoding A, B1, B2, or C Comprehension A, B, or C or REACH HIGHER	Fusion Reading or Read to Achieve (Taught by a regular LA teacher) Followed by Read to Achieve (must complete Fusion Reading first)			Regular Core Class	Honors Classes AP Classes Dual Credit Classes
Length of Time	2 Class Periods/day (In place of regular LAs)	1 Class Period/day in addition to a Regular LA. class Semester/Year			Semester/Year	Semester/Year
Verify Progress	Program assessments AIMS	Program assessments AIMS R-CBM and/or Maze			*Performance in Core coursework *Assessments *Grades	*Classroom performance *Rubrics on projects *Grades
Identify Method to Verify Effectiveness	*Percentage of students making adequate progress on AIMS in each support category					

Content Area Support and Motivation

> Make the clear distinction between intervention versus support.

A schoolwide and systems approach to RTI at the secondary level can and should include more than interventions for students with reading and math deficits; it should also include general support and a means of addressing student motivation. Schools should make a clear distinction between support and intervention. Too often, only support (help with homework, opportunities to redo work) is available to students who have specific skill deficits. Whereas generalized support may be necessary for some students, it is generally not sufficient for addressing specific reading or math skill deficits. Rather, support may be used in addition to intervention or effectively used for students without specific skill deficits. In both cases, schools would benefit by having a well-thought-out, organized plan for carrying out support. Such a plan can be designed both to provide academic support and to motivate students.

GOOD STANDING

Good Standing is conceptualized as a means of supporting and motivating students. A well-developed system in secondary schools should reduce the instances of student failure by providing extensive support. In fact, the overriding message of Good Standing should communicate the school culture is such that failure is not an acceptable option, or at the very minimum, difficult to achieve. In other words, failure should be more difficult for students than doing well. To fail, students have to overcome an extensive array of supports and consequences. The school's system is set up in such a way to encourage and support student academic success rather than simply using grades as the sole motivation for performance. Two examples of Good Standing are provided: one for middle school and one for high school.

Good Standing—Middle School

Riverton Middle School in Riverton, Wyoming, refer to their Good Standing approach as Spartan Time.

The Purpose of Spartan Time

1. Support students academically—immediately.

2. Motivate students to do their best—consistently.

Support:

Support Students Academically—as soon as they need it.

Provide specific and timely support *within* the school day.

Provide opportunity for students to redo work, make up work, and receive tutoring and intervention *before* instruction moves on to other topics.

Support provided by subject area teachers.

Motivate:

Consistently motivate students to do their best.

Motivate students by offering frequent and developmentally relevant rewards.

Rewards include fun, student-centered activities that allow opportunities to interact with peers—i.e., chess, quiz bowl, research, and quiet time.

What Happens in Spartan Time?

MONDAY: Students meet with scheduled Spartan Time teachers every Monday to check grades; contact parents; discuss RMS events, concerns, or issues that arise; or hold special events. (At the beginning of the year, students will be with their Spartan Time teacher every day until handbooks and beginning of the year activities are completed.)

TUESDAY, THURSDAY, FRIDAY: Students report to Spartan Time with their planner for attendance and announcements. Then students will go to one of the following:

1. Academic Assistance
2. Activities

Academic Assistance

How do students know if they must go to Academic Assistance?

Your teachers will mark your planner by circling the assignment you need to work on in your planner in Spartan Red on that day.

What subjects will we get help with during Academic Assistance?

Core classes (LA, Reading, Math, Social Studies, Science) will be the major focus; however, if caught up in core classes, you may need to catch up on exploratory assignments or projects.

Can I choose to go to Academic Assistance if I want to?

We encourage students to voluntarily come before they get behind. Students who want to come to work on school work, read AR books, and so on are welcome to attend.

Reasons for students to attend Academic Assistance:

- Complete assignments.
- Study for tests.
- Retake tests/quizzes.
- Ask about a confusing lesson or concept.
- Redo a poorly done assignment.
- Get make-up assignments.
- Work on projects (assigned, or History Day/Science Fair, etc.).

What do students going to Academic Assistance need to do?

- Arrive in the classroom on time with planner and materials.
- Make good use of the time and help.
- Always do your best.
- Show a positive attitude.
- Ask for help so you understand how to do your homework that night.
- Organize your homework to take home so you can complete it and go to activities the next day.
- Be prepared to stay in the classroom until 3:04 p.m. Read AR book if finished.

What will the Academic Assistance staff do to help students?

- Help students get organized with materials/planner.
- Monitor students' progress on assignments.
- Teach small group or individual lessons.
- Reinforce skills and concepts.
- Encourage goal setting by having students check grades on computer.
- Remind students of homework for the evening.
- Reward students who work hard in Academic Assistance for four days straight with a day of Activity Time.

Activity Time

What do students going to Activity Time need to do?

- Report to your grade-level activity area for that day, either the media center, gym, or multipurpose room. (Grade levels will be separated.)

- Use your unmarked planner for your pass to the area.
- Look at the options posted for the day.
- Choose the activity you want.
- Explore different types of activities that aren't available during the school day.
- Meet new staff and help plan fun activities you are interested in.
- Meet new friends with common interests.
- Celebrate your success.

What will the Activity Time staff do for the students?

- Plan variety of activities, for academic, physical, fun, and quiet areas.
- Post the activity choices and places where all can see (three-week rotation).
- Supervise activities.
- Vary activities according to student interest and participation.

Why are we doing this?

In the past we have provided after school opportunities for students to get academic help. Many students who needed help couldn't or wouldn't stay after school. Therefore, we decided to provide time during the day for them to get help. Students also said they wanted to have more free time, so students who complete their work successfully will be rewarded by having their choice of activities 3 times a week for about twenty minutes.

Can a student go to Activity Time without his or her planner?

No, that is the pass that shows the student has earned the activity.

What if I lose my planner?

If you don't find it, you may buy another for $5.00 in the office.

Does this take the place of our homeroom time?

Yes, but it is at the end of the day.

Source: Cheryl Mowry, Principal, Riverton Middle School.

Good Standing—High School

An example of Good Standing at the high school level includes Good Standing defined as *not failing.* Students not failing are in Good Standing; failing one or more classes results in mandatory after school tutoring in the subject area the student is failing—3:20 to 5:00 p.m. Monday is tutoring for English, Tuesday is for Math, Wednesday is for Science, and Thursday is for all other subjects. Friday is a make-up day for students who were unable to attend on their assigned day. Students failing only Math will attend Tuesdays. Students failing multiple classes must attend on all the days corresponding to the established schedule. Failure to attend after school results in mandatory Saturday School.

In addition to tutoring, students not in Good Standing must meet weekly with a mentor, complete a check-in/check-out form in which weekly performance in all classes is reviewed and discussed. Students must have the check-in form signed by all instructors indicating their weekly status.

Students can enter supports at any time during the nine weeks—each teacher is required to turn in a list of students failing at the end of day each Friday. Once a student is identified as not in Good Standing, he or she will immediately enter support class and continue in supports until the end of the nine weeks, during which time their status is reevaluated. If the student receives a failing grade, he or she will receive support for another nine weeks. If they are passing, the student is exited and monitored. Students remain in Good Standing as long as they are passing all classes.

RESEARCH-BASED
INTERVENTION AT THE SECONDARY LEVEL

- To develop a good decision-making process
- To develop an understanding of scientifically based research
- To investigate the research base of your programs and interventions
- To identify sources of information for evaluating effectiveness of programs
- To know your own context and needs
- To align interventions to student needs (Benchmark, Strategic, and Intensive)
- To monitor the extent to which they are effective

Education as Science

Education is science. And like other scientific fields, educational practices should be established on a knowledge base derived from

For every complex problem there is a simple solution . . . that doesn't work.

Proverb

Grades 9–12 "Good Standing" Placement

SCREENING	ACADEMIC PERFORMANCE (GRADES)			

↓ ↓ ↓ ↓

Diagnosis: Criteria	← Failing One or More Classes (Current or Previous Year) →			

↓ ↓ ↓ ↓

	Intensive	Strategic	Benchmark	Advanced
Focus:	← Academic Performance and / or Motivation →			
Intervene: Placement/Delivery	←	- Determine if skill deficits exist and address directly through direct instruction - Assign adult mentor - Assign afterschool tutoring for identified subject area(s) - Weekly check-in, check-out to monitor performance - Letter to parents - Contract with student - Late work agreement - Attendance plan and monitoring (as necessary)		→
Verify Progress: *Monitor response to intervention/instruction*	←	- Progress reviewed by mentor - Student report turned into office weekly - Grades - In-class performance - Good Standing reassessed at nine-week period		→
Certify Progress:	← Good-Standing performance in all coursework →			

scientific research. This applies not only to deciding what is taught, but also to all aspects of education, including how to structure schools, teaching methodologies, grading practices, managing behavior, polices regarding truancy, and grade retention.

Consider how educational decisions are often not science: anecdotal records, experience, and intuition, hearsay, trial and error, publisher's suggestions, nonexpert opinion, and, too often, the "cardiac method"—"I know in my heart" this is good for kids.

In effort to address struggling students, the not-so-distant past included the following practices with little empirical support regarding effectiveness:

- Neurological Processing and/or strengths and weaknesses
  - The focus is on remediating the process deficits, such as psycho-linguistic training.
- Modality-Matched and Multisensory
  - **Modality-Matched Approach.** Students have preferred modality, and teaching is matched to this modality (also called *learning styles*).
  - **Multisensory Instruction.** This method is aimed at using all pathways to the brain simultaneously, particularly visual, auditory, and kinesthetic.
- Cultural Learning Style
  - Assuming instruction can be tailored to specific cultures

Why Scientifically Based Research?

Reason 1: Short- and Long-Term Consequences

Perhaps the most compelling reason is that educators want what works. Administrators and teachers understand all too well the consequences and costs of unsuccessful programs. Secondary teachers can vouch for the long-term implications for students who leave elementary school without essential skills in reading and math.

Reason 2: Learning That Failure Is Preventable

At all levels, educators are coming to terms with the fact that many learning difficulties are preventable and even fixable—if attention is paid to the right factors and we are prepared to act. We understand research can guide instructional practices and actions to help maximize limited resources and time, aligning odds in favor of successful outcomes. We also understand what is at stake and the role we play in the lives of students.

Reason 3: Increased Accountability

Using scientifically based research also receives greater emphasis because of increased accountability:

- More accountability for increasing academic achievement of all students, especially those most in need

- Increased attention to program integrity leading to clear theories of action and procedural guidelines of proven effectiveness
- To demonstrate that local programs are grounded in a theory of action and conceptual rationale that links activities to results

APPLYING SCIENTIFICALLY BASED RESEARCH TO EDUCATION

What Is Scientifically Based Research in Education?

- **Sound Methods.** The research is based on standard methods of collecting reliable and valid data to ensure consistency across studies.
- **Experimental Design.** The research is evaluated using experimental or quasi-experimental designs with a preference for random-assignment experiments and within-conditions or across-conditions controls.
- **Clearly Specified.** The research is presented in sufficient detail and clarity to allow for replication and further study.
- **Peer Review.** The research has been accepted by a peer-reviewed journal or approved by a panel of independent experts.

What Are the Key Considerations When Reviewing Studies of Educational Programs or Practices? Ask:

1. Has the study been published in a peer-reviewed journal or approved by a panel of independent experts?

2. Have the results of the study been replicated by others?

3. Is there consensus in the research community that the study's findings are supported by a critical mass of additional studies?

What Are the Elements of an Effective Instructional Approach?

Explicit Instructional Strategies. Teachers must be provided with instructions on what and how they are to teach the material included in the selected intervention program. This ensures consistency across classrooms and among teachers and improves fidelity.

Coordinated Instructional Sequences. The intervention program builds on previously acquired skills, reinforces progress, and provides extensive repetition, a practice well-grounded in brain research (Medina, 2008).

Ample Practice Opportunities. Students need a variety of types of practice from seeing the skill modeled, scaffolded, and guided practice. Repeated trials and drill opportunities to apply skills and/or knowledge while solving problems and analyzing and synthesizing.

Aligned Student Materials. Assessment and curriculum, practice and activities, and outcome measures must be consistent and interrelated.

What Instructional Approaches Yield Significant Outcomes for Struggling Students? Approaches That

- Include modeling
- Are well specified
- Are structured and systematic
- Are explicit
- Are carefully designed
- Are closely related to the area of instructional need
- Include repetition
- Provide guided and controlled opportunities for practice
- Scaffold learning supports
- Include corrective and immediate feedback

Consider... If there is a lack of information about a particular program, emphasis should be placed on its instructional design. Does it make use of explicit teaching, modeling, guided practice, gradual release, and so on? If not, caution is advised.

What Are the Criteria for Intervention Program Efficacy?

- Does the program have evidence of efficacy established through carefully designed experimental studies?
- Was the program tested in schools with similar demographic and learner profiles as your school?
- Does the program reflect current and confirmed research?
- Does the program provide explicit, systematic instruction in well-recognized reading and math dimensions including:

Reading	Math
Phonics	Number and operations
Decoding	Algebra
Word recognition	Geometry
Spelling	Measurement
Comprehension (listening and reading)	Data analysis and probability
Vocabulary	Problem solving and estimation
Writing	Reasoning and proof
Oral and written communication	Communication
	Connections
	Representation

Remember to look for

- independent peer review (Not all education journals are peer-reviewed.),
- replication of results by other studies, and
- consensus within a research community.

Intervention Cannot Be Optional

Above all, at the secondary level, intervention cannot be viewed as optional. We must begin with the notion that we are obligated to act if and when students do not have the skills necessary to be successful. We must view intervention as something that does not require parental consent and as something that students cannot opt out of. In contrast, schools must communicate why interventions are provided and explain to parents, and especially students, how they work and what students will gain as a result of the intervention process. Intervention must be viewed as a partnership between the school, families, and the student. Intervention at the secondary level is a beneficial service, similar to what parents would pay an outside tutoring service such as Sylvan Learning Center.

YOUR TURN

RESEARCH-BASED INTERVENTIONS—ACTIVITY 2

1. How do your school's reading and math intervention programs adhere to the criteria described so far in this chapter? What specific sources can you identify that support your school's core reading and math core programs and instruction?

2. To what degree do other policies and practices within your school adhere to principles of scientifically based research? Consider policies and practices such as grade retention, grading policies, attendance policies, and so on.

WHAT EXACTLY IS AN INTERVENTION?

Exactly what constitutes an intervention, let alone an effective research-based/validated intervention, has previously been an elusive pursuit at for many secondary schools. There is confusion between interventions and accommodations/modifications. There is also a lack of clear guidelines and criteria for judging intervention quality. For certain, not all interventions are created equal, and this must be a guiding premise for secondary schools as they undertake the challenge of selecting interventions on the behalf of students with skill deficiencies—students for whom traditional instruction has not been successful. It must be recognized that secondary students in need of intervention have often had skill deficits since grade school and, despite previous intervention attempts, remain academically challenged due to poor basic reading, writing, and math skills. Educators of secondary students are encouraged to read Interventions for Adolescent Struggling Readers by Scammacca et al. (2007) (www.centeroninstruction.org).

- Interventions are:
  - Linked to a goal—the behavior and/or performance will change relative to the goal set by the team;
  - Systematic/planful—the procedures to be applied are specified clearly and completely; and
  - Environmentally focused—the actions taken modify the environment, not only the student.

- Intervention is an action that directly develops or improves a skill.

  Examples of intervention include:
  - Directly teaching (modeling, scaffolding, providing feedback) students to decode words using advanced word analysis;
  - Directly teaching specific strategies for sentence writing;
  - Directly teaching multiple-digit division; and
  - Improving comprehension by directly teaching students to generate questions, find main ideas and important details, paraphrasing, and summarizing

- Interventions require:
  - Specifically focused intervention classes;
  - A minimum of forty-five minutes per day;
  - Small homogeneous group instruction;
  - Extended duration—months or years; and
  - A systematic approach that includes effective instructional strategies (explicit instruction, modeling, scaffolding, multiple opportunities to respond, controlled opportunity for practice, corrective feedback, systematic error correction).

- Interventions are **NOT** accommodations **OR** adaptations.
  - Accommodations are supports or services provided to help a student access the general curriculum (e.g., accepting oral responses to a history test, using large print, or allowing more time to complete assignments).
  - Adaptations are changes made to the content and performance expectations for students (e.g., different and/or simplified vocabulary, below grade-level math standards, or simplified concepts).

Because accommodations and adaptations are not interventions, this does not lessen their necessity and utility for struggling students. In fact, most students receiving interventions, especially intense level interventions, will require accommodations or adaptations or both until the student's skill or performance level is sufficiently improved to allow for independent functioning. Secondary teachers must be trained and supported as they identify ways to accommodate and provide adaptions for older students will skill deficits. The concept of mainstream Consultation Agreements (Tindal, Shinn, Walz, & Germann, 1987) could easily be applied to groups of students with similar skill deficits and accommodation needs.

LINKING INTERVENTION AND INSTRUCTIONAL TIERS

Students are placed in the level of support they require to acquire grade-level core knowledge and essential skills in language arts and math. Consider the three levels of instructional support:

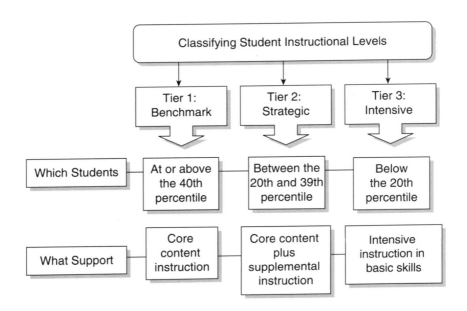

The above illustration is similar to the familiar three-tier pyramid, where support is aligned to student instructional needs. In contrast to the traditional pyramid, however, the above concept matches supports to student instructional needs but does not assign Tier 3 to special education. Rather, special education students, like all students, vary in their need for support depending on existing skill sets in reading, writing, math, behavior, and so on. In other words, any student could be considered as a candidate for Tier 3/Intensive supports if his or her skills in a particular area place him or her below the 20th percentile. In further contrast to the RTI pyramid, tiered intervention is provided to all students who fall into a particular tier and require intervention, which may be more than 5 to 10 percent of the student population. Thus, If 17 percent of sixth graders have reading skills below the 20th percentile, then 16 percent of sixth graders could be provided intensive reading intervention. If an unusually high percentage of students require reading intervention, consideration should be given to evaluating the appropriateness of core reading programs and instruction at the lower grades. Often, a high percentage of students requiring intensive supports is a sign the core reading, math, or writing instructional materials are not effective and/or a good match for your student population. Is a program that has limited modeling, scaffolding, and explicit instruction being used with a student population that requires lots of structure? If so, more appropriate core programs and improved core instruction could reduce the need for intervention later. Nevertheless, the current sixth-grade students with reading deficits are going to require intervention now. More appropriate core instruction could reduce this incidence for the future, which is why secondary schools should have a strong interest in the effectiveness of elementary programs.

WHY USE INTERVENTION PROGRAMS?

Simply put, programs are tools. Virtually every profession seeks effective tools to assist in achieving a final product. In education, intervention programs are teaching tools that are implemented by teachers to increase the odds of achieving academic outcomes. A well-designed intervention program is specially and carefully planned to teach critical elements. Skills are introduced, learned, reviewed, assessed, repeated, and expanded. Program effectiveness is determined by how well they are designed and coordinate instruction (scope and sequence) and, most important, their approach to instruction (instructional design).

Consider the scope and sequence of a middle and high school math intervention program—Essentials for Algebra. It illustrates the difficulty teachers face if they find themselves in the position of teaching all the pre-algebra skills to students with deficits without an intervention program. Not only would they have to account for everything that would need to be covered and the sequence of skills and/or concepts, but they would also face an even more daunting task of ensuring the instructional mistakes of the past are not repeated. They would have to possess expert knowledge regarding instructional design and how to match it to the characteristics of struggling learners. For secondary students with skill deficits, the most important consideration may not be what to teach, but how to teach in a way consistent with how struggling students learn. In short, teachers would have to ensure each lesson adhered to the following critical principles of instruction:

GENERAL FEATURES OF INSTRUCTION

1. Instructor models instructional tasks when appropriate.

- ❑ Demonstrates the task (e.g., uses think alouds)
- ❑ Proceeds in step-by-step fashion
- ❑ Limits language to demonstration of skill
- ❑ Makes eye contact with students, speaks clearly while modeling skill

2. Instructor provides explicit instruction.

- ❑ Sets the purpose for the instruction
- ❑ Identifies the important details of the concept being taught
- ❑ Provides instructions that have only one interpretation
- ❑ Makes connection to previously learned material

3. Instructor engages students in meaningful interactions with language during lesson.

- ❑ Provides and elicits background information
- ❑ Emphasizes distinctive features of new concepts
- ❑ Uses visuals and manipulatives to teach content as necessary
- ❑ Makes relationships among concepts overt
- ❑ Engages students in discourse around new concepts
- ❑ Elaborates on student responses

4. Instructor provides multiple opportunities for students to practice instructional tasks.

- ❑ Provides more than one opportunity to practice each new skill
- ❑ Provides opportunities for practice after each step in instruction
- ❑ Elicits group responses when feasible
- ❑ Provides extra practice based on accuracy of student responses

5. Instructor provides corrective feedback after initial student responses.

- ❑ Provides affirmations for correct responses
- ❑ Promptly corrects errors with provision of correct model

❑ Limits corrective feedback language to the task at hand

❑ Ensures mastery of all students before moving on

6. Students are engaged in the lesson during teacher-led instruction.

❑ Gains student attention before initiating instruction

❑ Paces lesson to maintain attention

❑ Maintains close proximity to students

❑ Transitions quickly between tasks

❑ Intervenes with off-task students to maintain their focus

7. Students are engaged in the lesson during independent work.

❑ Independent work routines and procedures previously taught

❑ Models task before allowing students to work independently

❑ Checks for student understanding of the task(s)

❑ Students use previously learned strategies or routines when they come to a task they don't understand

❑ Independent work is completed with high level of accuracy

8. Students are successful completing activities at a high criterion level of performance.

❑ Elicits a high percentage of accurate responses from group

❑ Elicits a high percentage of accurate responses from individuals

❑ Holds same standard of accuracy for high performers and low performers

9. Instructor encourages student effort.

❑ Provides feedback during and after task completion

❑ Provides specific feedback about student's accuracy and/or effort

❑ Majority of feedback is positive

❑ Celebrates or displays examples of student success in reading

Source: Robinson, J. (2009, March), Oregon Reading First: Cohort B Leadership Session, Center on Teaching and Learning (CTL), University of Oregon. Portland, OR. Used with permission.

UNDERSTANDING THE PURPOSES
OF DIFFERENT INTERVENTION PROGRAMS

Types of Intervention Programs

Targeted Programs are programs and materials that are designed to target and improve specific skills, such as instruction in one or more areas of reading (phonics/word analysis, comprehension). Targeted programs can be effective in improving a student's overall reading level by improving his or her skill in a particular area. For example, if a student has difficulty decoding multisyllable words, the program Rewards could be used to target and/or improve advanced word decoding, thereby improving overall reading and comprehension.

Targeted programs

- target and improve the critical skills required in reading, writing, and math;
- provide more instruction or practice in particular area(s) of need;
- might include large group, small group; and
- provide explicit and systematic instruction, modeling, scaffolding, careful monitoring, and feedback.

Comprehensive Programs provide instruction to students performing below grade level on multiple skills (such as, phonic awareness, phonics, fluency, vocabulary, and comprehension). Comprehensive intervention is typically delivered in smaller, homogeneous group settings, but can be the whole class if students are placed with similarly skilled students.

> The bottom 20 to 25 percent of students will require a very different kind of effort in both the short and long run if they are to meet grade-level standards.

Comprehensive intervention programs can be and often are used as a replacement to the core instruction (example: Hampton Brown Edge or Language! programs are used in place of English!). Special consideration must be given to graduation requirements for students receiving intervention at the high school level. For students with severe deficits, alternate graduation requirements should be considered and are often planned as part of a student's IEP (individualized education program). At minimum, elective credit can be given for completion of intervention classes. Secondary educators should also identify, when possible, if content could be added to the intervention so it would meet State requirements for graduation credit. The program Essentials for Algebra, for example, is considered a pre-algebra program. By adding approximately sixty days of additional content to Essentials for Algebra's existing 120 lessons, it would meet Algebra 1 standards and thus count as Algebra 1 credit.

Comprehensive intervention programs are

- designed for students who demonstrate difficulty and are performing significantly below grade level;
- provide more explicit, systematic instruction to *accelerate* learning and to bring the learner closer to grade-level performance;
- have a high criterion level of performance;
- typically focus on multiple areas (such as, phonics, fluency, and comprehension);
- specialized, intense, and typically delivered in smaller group settings; and
- often include placement tests, mastery checks, and an acceleration schedule.

Where to Find Reviews of Existing Secondary level Interventions

- rti4success
- WWC
- Slavin's BEE

Interventions That Work for Older Students (my biased list)

Comprehensive Reading Interventions

1. Reach Higher (Corrective Reading, Reasoning and Writing, Morphographic Spelling)

2. Language!

3. Read 180

4. The Reading Edge

5. Wilson Reading

Strategic Reading Interventions

1. Rewards (multisyllable decoding)

2. Read to Achieve (comprehension strategies)

Math

1. Essentials for Algebra
2. Corrective Math
3. Trans Math

One finding from all research is that a comprehensive instructional program is necessary to ensure that intervention does not lead to splintered understanding that interferes in the development of essential skills and conceptual knowledge.

Combine the purpose of the program with the appropriate support level.

Tier 2 Versus Tier 3

Tier 2 Interventions	Tier 3 Interventions
• 20th to 39th percentile	• Below 20th percentile
• Targeted skills	• Comprehensive focus
• In addition to core class	• Often in place of core class
• Embedded within class or additional period per day	• Use of published intervention programs

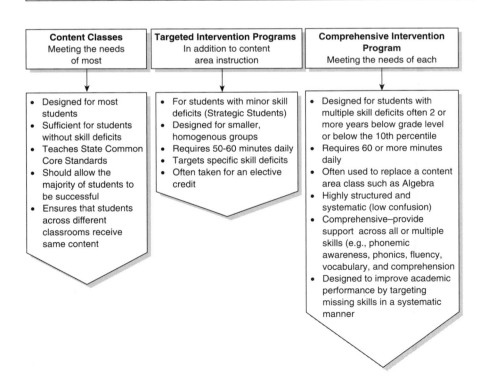

YOUR TURN

RESEARCH-BASED INTERVENTIONS—ACTIVITY 3

1. Identify the programs currently being used in your building for strategic and intensive students. Are they well matched to student needs?

2. Are they research validated?

3. Do they meet the criterion outlined in this chapter regarding structure and how skills are taught?

4. Are interventions implemented with fidelity and for an extended period of time (months or even years)?

Beyond matching research-validated interventions to students' instructional needs, a host of other factors must be considered if secondary intervention systems are to be effective. Presented below are six additional considerations to improve outcomes for secondary students receiving academic interventions.

1. Increased Leadership

A representative leadership team will

- hold monthly meetings to establish, evaluate, and problem solve intervention systems;
- use data as the basis for discussions and decisions;
- use research as the basis for decision making;
- use effective decision-making procedures and group operating principles; and
- create pathways for systematically providing necessary interventions in reading, math, writing, and behavior.

2. Create Data Collection and Data Analysis Systems

An effective data collection and data analysis system requires

- a plan to administer, score, share, and analyze screening and progress-monitoring data;
- a lead staff guided by a principal or coach to analyze data at monthly departmental or RTI level teams;
- revisions in interventions, grouping, and the established placement pathway plan that are based on data analysis; and
- adjustments in classroom instruction based on data analysis.

3. Maximize Time

To be effective, intervention must be of sufficient length, intensity, and duration. This includes

- the typical recommendation for secondary intervention classes is forty-five to sixty minutes per day;
- an additional thirty to forty-five minutes of instruction for interventions that recommend ninety minutes per day; and
- additional instruction time for students requiring preteaching, teaching, additional opportunities for practice, and so on.

4. Group Students to Optimize Learning

It is important to emphasize that flexible skill grouping is not tracking. Flexible skill groups are based on a student's skills and instructional needs. They are designed with consideration given to pacing to ensure outcomes and timelines are targeted and reached. Students are regrouped as necessary to not hold back a student who could move faster with the group and, likewise, to offer the option to regroup a student to a lower group to meet his or her needs and not sacrifice the group for an individual student.

To optimize learning

- provide instruction aligned with student needs—use diagnostic assessment to identify targets,
- use creative and flexible grouping to maximize performance,
- organize groups small enough to closely monitor student responses during all phases of instruction,
- be flexible, base decisions on data,
- review performance at regular intervals (twice monthly), and
- vary the pace and level of instruction to meet pacing and progress goals.

High quality differentiated instruction includes

- differentiating instruction for each student so all students can reach their academic goals. Differentiation requires changing what is taught, how it is taught, and how students practice;
- varying the intensity, amount, explicitness, and response requirements;
- teaching each child to high criterion levels of performance;
- reviewing previously taught material before introducing new material; and
- monitoring student performance during and after instruction.

To differentiate instruction

- use data to identify students who need additional or substantial instruction;
- use progress-monitoring data to adjust instruction;
- when possible, select supplemental and intervention programs that complement one another; and
- manipulate "alterable variables" to intensify instruction. Alternate variables include increasing direct teaching, modeling, feedback, time, and practice.

5. Staff Appropriately

Quality teaching requires a well-organized structure and a supportive work environment. To maximize learning for secondary students receiving intervention

- use staff with the most skills and expertise in research-based reading and math interventions;
- provide ongoing training, coaching, and support to teachers in effective instructional techniques; and
- train additional staff in scientific reading and math interventions.

6. Parent and Family Involvement for Students Placed in Interventions

It is important that parents become a meaningful partner in the implementation of interventions, the data collected to demonstrate progress, and the need to select less or more intensive instructional or behavioral strategies.

A school should provide written progress-monitoring data to parents on a routine basis. In addition, parents must receive ongoing and precise information regarding their student's interventions, response to the interventions, and progress toward intervention goals. This information should include

- The student's need
- A description of the specific intervention and who is delivering instruction
- Clearly stated intervention goals and academic progress expected for their student
- How often progress will be monitored
- How adequate or insufficient progress will be determined
- The date(s) progress will be reviewed
- How the intervention class(es) will impact the student's graduation
- The right to request a special education evaluation at any time

CONCLUSION

Talented secondary teachers, even specially trained teachers, may not necessarily have the knowledge and skills to remediate students with skill deficits. By middle and high school, students with reading and math deficits have likely received well-intended attempts to make them better readers and/or math students. Secondary schools must recognize that such students require specially designed, research-validated interventions made specifically for older students. Teachers cannot be expected to create or write such instruction and must be equipped with the professional tools and supporting structure to adequately address student needs. This chapter outlines ways to create effective intervention systems for struggling students as well as ways to improve core instruction for all students. The next chapter addresses how assessments are used to inform instruction, including diagnostic assessments as well as progress monitoring. The window for improving essential skills is very small for secondary students. They simply cannot afford well-intended yet ineffective interventions.

Blank worksheets and user forms discussed in this chapter are available for download at **www.partnersforlearning.org**.

Data-Based Decision Making

4

OBJECTIVES:

- Understand the four purposes of assessment
- Know the importance of establishing a building-level assessment plan
- Know the benefits of using CBMs as part of a comprehensive measurement system at the secondary level
- Understand how CBMs can be used to fulfill specific assessment purposes
- Know the importance of using a data management system for easy organization and interpretation of data
- Be able to establish progress monitoring at the secondary level

Although the idea of using data for instructional decision making receives a lot of attention, few schools or educators feel this is something they do particularly well. In truth, assessments too often do not lend themselves to be used for formative decision making. They take too long to administer, are expensive, and often do not provide information that is instructionally relevant. Likewise, schools often are not set up to use data in a direct and systematic fashion. They often see results as being indicative of their students rather than a reflection of the effectiveness of systems and instruction.

This chapter is designed to help schools build a plan for instructional decision making. The overriding goal is to (1) identify data sources that are easy and time efficient to administer and score, (2) establish powerful ways to summarize and display data for easy interpretation, and (3) create a format to allow data to be analyzed and used for instructional decision making and planning.

Batsche et al. (2005) identified four components of an effective assessment system, which are as follows:

1. A comprehensive measurements system that addresses the multiple purposes of assessment

2. A data management system that summarizes the data in easy-to-interpret reports

3. A formative decision-making model

4. A *communication plan* for data analyses and instructional decision-making

COMPONENT ONE: A COMPREHENSIVE MEASUREMENT SYSTEM THAT ADDRESSES THE MULTIPLE PURPOSES OF ASSESSMENT

What: Schools implementing a systems approach to RTI require assessments for specific purposes, including (1) identifying which students require additional instructional supports, (2) answering the question, what skills need to be taught, and (3) measuring if and to what degree instructional supports are effective.

How: A comprehensive assessment plan developed by each school specifying what assessments will be used to guide instructional decision making. As part of a comprehensive measurement system, the following should be considered:

A. Understand the Purposes of Assessment

Consider the purposes of assessments and how each serves to inform instructional decision making.

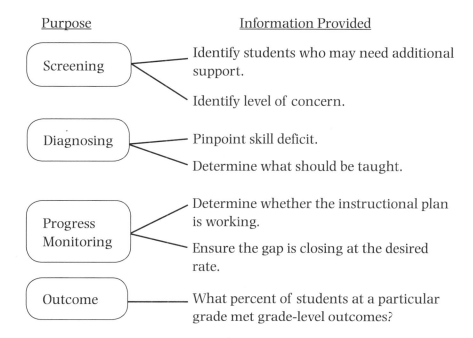

Purpose	Information Provided

Screening — Identify students who may need additional support. Identify level of concern.

Diagnosing — Pinpoint skill deficit. Determine what should be taught.

Progress Monitoring — Determine whether the instructional plan is working. Ensure the gap is closing at the desired rate.

Outcome — What percent of students at a particular grade met grade-level outcomes?

B. Develop a Building-Level Assessment Plan

Develop a plan for collecting and using data relative to the four purposes of assessment. In developing an assessment plan

- each school/district will identify an assessment team;
- assessment teams will specify what assessment data will be obtained, when and how it will be disseminated and used; and
- the RTI team, departmental teams, Professional Learning Communities (PLCS), and individual-student teams will use the data for instructional decision making.

The assessment plan for secondary schools should

1. Specify what assessments and criterion will be used to identify students in need of additional, more in-depth assessments.

2. Establish criteria for determining whether students are at grade level (Benchmark), below grade level (Strategic), or significantly below grade level (Intensive).

3. Assess (using diagnostic testing) to determine student instructional needs. Many published intervention programs include program specific placement tests.

4. Monitor progress according to level of concern: Strategic—once a month; Intensive—every two weeks.

5. Specify how data will be used to evaluate the effectiveness of instructional supports and guide adjustments to the plan (that is, during monthly departmental meetings, PLCS, and the format to efficiently organize data walls, and so on).

C. Using Curriculum-Based Measurement (CBM) as Part of a Comprehensive Measurement System

Before discussing the benefits of using Curriculum-Based Measurements (CBMs) at the secondary school level, it is important to acknowledge and emphasize that most middle and high schools already have assessments that can be used for many of the same purposes that CBMs serve, especially screening students to identify those at risk and candidates for intervention. For example, State assessments, Measurement of Academic Progress (MAP), and ACT Testing results can serve as great indicators regarding which students may be in trouble. CBMs can be used in conjunction with existing assessments for the purpose of confirming or ruling out whether students do indeed have skill deficits requiring intervention. They can also provide additional insight about the nature of the academic difficulties (e.g., decoding vs. comprehension) and, most important, be used to monitor the progress of students receiving intervention. An in-depth discussion of CBMs and how they can be used at the secondary level is presented below.

Curriculum-Based Measurement (CBM) is well-suited for use in a comprehensive measurement system. The measurements are time efficient and easily administered; they provide reliable and valid information relevant to screening, diagnosing, monitoring progress, and predicting outcomes. In short, CBMs meet the requirements of good assessment.

What are the qualities of good assessment?

- Facilitates instructional decision making
- Easily administered, scored, and interpreted
- Measures skills that are important and predictive of academic success
- Fits within day-to-day instructional routines
- Valid and reliable

Q and A About CBMs: What Are the Big Ideas of CBMs?

CBMs are intended to be a measure of a student's development of basic skills. They are not intended to measure everything that could be assessed regarding student learning. Rather, they provide brief, but accurate insight into how well essential skills are developing—skills predictive of current and future academic success.

CBM as DIBS

D *Dynamic*	I *Indicator*	BS *Basic Skills*
Indicates sensitivity to differences Sensitive between—detects differences between children Sensitive within—detects incremental change in performance within a student over time	Indicator of academic health Indicators of essential academic skills. Similar to vital signs of health (blood pressure, temperature, heart rate, and so on) Not the only indicator or measurement that could be used Doesn't measure everything . . . not intended to	Measures basic skills Skills necessary for and predictive of academic success Reading (phonics, fluency, comprehension) Spelling Mathematics Written expression Foundation Skills (vocabulary, alliteration, rhyming, phonemic awareness) Early Literacy Skills

What Purposes Can CBMs Serve?

Consider the utility of CBM within the framework of the four purposes of assessment. CBMs are efficient, valid measures that can be used in conjunction with other assessments to guide important decisions about the effectiveness of systems as well as for individual students.

CBM and Purpose of Assessment

Purpose of Assessment	*Valid Measure*
Screening	Yes
Diagnostic	Partial-error analysis
Progress monitoring	Yes
Outcome measure	Yes

Are CBMs Accurate Measures?

CBMs are valid, reliable, and predictive of academic success. They are available from various commercial publishers, including the following: AIMSweb (aimsweb.com), DIBELS, EasyCBM, Intervention Central, and FAST (Formative Assessment System for Teachers).

How Can CBM Results Be Used?

The data gathered from curriculum-based measurement can be used for multiple purposes beyond assessing individual students. In fact, when used as part of a systems approach, CBMs are an important part of evaluating effectiveness. In the evaluation chapter, information will be provided on how CBMs can be used by departmental or RTI teams to evaluate if systems are healthy. Emphasis is placed on system effectiveness before looking at individual students. Student concerns are often a by-product of ineffective systems that go unnoticed and, more important, unchallenged. CBMs are also used to

- identify how many students require instructional supports;
- identify the level of instructional supports necessary for students;
- develop small groups for specialized strategies or interventions;
- set goals for systems;
- set goals for instructional groups;
- set goals for individual students;
- monitor progress and determine intervention effectiveness;
- assess new students to your school and provide appropriate instructional placement;
- task analyze student skills;
- provide parents or guardians with regular "report cards" on progress relative to goals, interventions, or classmates; and
- evaluate the effectiveness of support systems within intervention classes, departments, schools, or districts.

Remember . . . When Establishing a Comprehensive Assessment System:

DO	DON'T
Use assessments with a high degree of reliability and validity.	Rely on assessments that are overly time-consuming and therefore unlikely to be sustained.
Use assessments that can serve multiple purposes (screening, progress monitoring, predicting outcomes, and so on).	Use assessments without established reliability and validity.

DO	DON'T
Use assessments that are easy and time-efficient to administer.	Use multiple assessments for the same purpose; pick one that is highly predictive of results you would get from using multiple assessments.
Use assessments that are easy to interpret and instructionally relevant.	Administer assessments without using them for instructional decision making.
Use assessments that are sustainable across classrooms, across learning environments, and across time (grade to grade).	Collect data without a specific reason.

YOUR TURN

Data Systems

Consider what assessments are currently used in your building for Reading and Math. Complete the table below. Then answer the following questions:

1. Are multiple assessments being used for the same purpose?

2. How much time is spent conducting various assessments and how well is the information used for instructional decision making?

3. Are there assessments that you do not know or cannot confirm evidence of reliability and validity?

4. Are additional assessments necessary? If so, what assessments?

	Assessment Name	Grade	Purpose of assessment	Evidence of reliability and validity?	How are the data used for instructional decision making?
R E A D I N G					

(Continued)

(Continued)

	Assessment Name	Grade	Purpose of assessment	Evidence of reliability and validity?	How are the data used for instructional decision making?
M					
A					
T					
H					

COMPONENT TWO: A DATA MANAGEMENT SYSTEM THAT SUMMARIZES THE DATA IN EASY TO INTERPRET REPORTS

What: The goal is to have a clear plan for collecting and using data for specific instructional decision making purposes. Closer examination, however, reveals data are often not well used, not because there is a lack of data or that educators don't want to use data, but because they are too often presented in formats that are not useful or difficult to interpret. If teachers are required to use data but have to spend extensive time searching through piles of confusing reports, this greatly reduces the likelihood they will be consistently employed for decision making.

How: Most CBM data systems (EasyCBM, AIMSweb, FAST) use report formats that are generally easy to understand and interpret. The example AIMSweb report provided below is an illustration. It identifies each student's score, percentile, risk status, and Instructional Recommendation. For each class as well as grade, it identifies the percent of students requiring instructional supports and the level of support. Results can also be used to evaluate system effectiveness discussed in Chapter 6, Problem Solving to Achieve Effective Outcomes—Systems and Students.

Universal Screening

Student Name	Student Score	Percentile Score	Instructional Recommendation
Joe Smith	120	50	Core Instruction
Sara Jones	75	10	Needs Intervention

Data reports like the one above are readily available through various web-based data systems such as EasyCBM, AIMSweb, and so on. They are easy to access and relatively inexpensive, especially when compared with other data systems that often use measures not applicable to ongoing progress monitoring.

Although it is beyond the scope of this chapter to present all the various reports that are available for reporting data, one data system, Kidgraph, is highlighted because of its unique approach to tracking student performance. Kidgraph is unique in that both in-program as well as out-of-program (CBM) monitoring is summarized on one page, and emphasis given to tracking instructional groups. The group focus allows educators to evaluate the effectiveness of the instruction itself, first asking, "is it working for the majority of the students in the group?" while also tracking the performance of individual students. Below are the unique features of Kidgraph as related to data-based decision making. It is presented again in Chapter 6 as a means of evaluating and problem-solving systems.

Features of Kidgraph

Kidgraph is an electronic or paper/pencil data summary and organization form that assesses learning by incorporating in-program and out-of-program assessments to ensure students not only learn program content but also are able to apply newly acquired skills to everyday learning (e.g., apply newly acquired phonic skills to read a grade-level passage or apply comprehension strategies when reading passages not directly related to interventions). The question in such instances being answered is whether students are able to transfer newly acquired skills to tasks outside of the specific teaching context.

Kidgraph:

Monitors learning at the instructional group and individual student levels.

- Individual student performance is tracked and displayed electronically but viewed in the context of and in comparison to the instructional group.
- Places emphasis on the instructional group; Kidgraph changes the perspective from student characteristics to evaluating effectiveness of instruction (program, instruction, and teacher effectiveness).

Creates pacing maps (amount of content to be taught).

- Requires planning and tracking of instructional pacing.
- This ensures students learn adequate amounts of content required to close the achievement gap.

Maximizes the potential of instructional programs.

- Provides information of whether (a) enough content is being covered, (b) students are firm in skills taught, and (c) students are generalizing newly acquired skills.
- Helps pinpoint what to modify when students aren't learning or aren't learning enough. Kidgraph provides evaluation at both the group and individual student level so instructional adjustments can be applied accordingly.

Provides a graphic display of data as they are entered using easy to interpret color coding.

- Provides immediate data feedback.
- Allows for easy and powerful tracking and interpretation of student learning. Provides a visual that can be used to
  - o evaluate effectiveness of instruction at the systems, group, and individual student level;
  - o improve use of data for decision making;
  - o establish and maintain focus during instructional planning meetings;

- o increase focus to instructional pacing;
- o ensure students are appropriately grouped;
- o document changes to interventions; and
- o evaluate and improve program fidelity.

Is uniquely suited for RTI.

- Provides information relative to a student's intervention history, including: a list of interventions applied and completed, comprehensive tracking of in-program performance, pacing, amount of content completed, performance on out-of-program monitoring (e.g., easyCBM), days absent, and a performance comparison to the instructional group.
- Can be used in conjunction with virtually all instructional programs (e.g., Read to Achieve, Corrective Reading, etc.) and applied to any size instructional group.

Is easy to use.

- Data are easily entered within minutes by teachers or teacher assistants
  - o Data entered are the same data already collected as part of daily instruction.
  - o Data can be entered and/or transferred from other sources such as easyCBM or AIMSweb.
  - o Once entered, data are instantly summarized for instructional decision making.
  - o Groups can be easily manipulated and updated as students move in and out of flexible groups.

To purchase Kidgraph or to find out more, go to Partnersforlearning. org or contact Partners for Learning, Inc. (208) 322–5007.

COMPONENT THREE: A FORMATIVE DECISION-MAKING MODEL

What: Using data to inform instructional decisions

How: The Assessment-Intervention Loop

Kidgraph Tracking Form: Middle School

Monitoring Instructional Groups
Kidgraph Form 1

Group Instructor: Beck   **Program: Corrective Reading B-1**

Grade/Group: 6th – Gray   **Date: 10/15/09**

Expected Lesson#_ 113

Actual Lesson #_ 107

Student Name	Passed Mastery Tests?	On Aimline?		Behavior +/-	Days Absent	Comments:
Javaris	Y	Y		+	2	
Willy	Y	Y		+	0	
Jamal	N	Y		+	4	Failed last 2 mastery tests; passed re-tests
Leticia	Y	Y		+	1	
Jani	N	N		+	0	Passed re-test
Duane	Y	Y		+	0	
Devon	Y	Y		+	0	
Marrisa	N	Y		+	2	Passed all previous mastery tests
Kimberly	Y	Y		-	0	
Anthony	Y	Y		+	0	
Toni	Y	Y		+	1	
Alee	Y	Y		+	0	
% of students Passing/ on Aimline?	83%	92%				

Although we may not realize it, formative decision making is used continuously in other aspects of our daily lives. For instance, when inspecting a garden, you are looking to make sure everything is progressing as anticipated. You use visual data and expectations of growth to identify plants that need additional support (screening). From here you take a closer look at the plants identified during screening to better understand the reason behind the lack of progress (diagnostic testing). Is it too little or too much water, not enough sunshine, too much sunshine, too much not enough fertilizer, overcrowding, insects, disease? What is causing the problem? Using the data obtained through inspection and a quick visit to the Internet, you identify the problem and this informs the remedy (intervention). You then develop a plan for carrying out the necessary remedy. From here you make frequent checks to ensure the remedy is having the desired outcome (progress monitoring). If all goes well, your efforts result in terrific tasting salad and possibly a trip to the state fair. If not, it's off to the supermarket.

Unfortunately, for students, the stakes are much higher than a trip to the supermarket. If your efforts are not successful, the consequences of not having adequate language, reading, and math skills are devastating and last a lifetime.

The assessment-intervention loop incorporates these decision-making steps:

1. **Identify need for support** by defining goals of expected performance—how much by when.

2. **Define and validate the need for support** required to meet expected levels of performance.

3. **Explore and plan instructional intervention** to meet student needs.

4. **Look and review results** to ensure instructional supports are effective.

Step 1.

> **What:** Identify need for support by defining goals of expected performance—how much by when.
>
> **How:** Screening, comparing performance to established standards.

Screening Assessment/Universal Screening

Assessment	Purpose
Screening	**Identify students in need of instructional support**
	Validate level of support required
Diagnostic	Used to provide more in-depth analysis of a student's strengths and weaknesses to guide instruction
Progress Monitoring	Used to ensure that a student is on track and for making course corrections
Outcome	End of year benchmark testing used to determine what percentage of students at a particular grade met grade-level outcomes

Universal Screening

As part of a systems approach to RTI, secondary schools must have a means to identify quickly and accurately where students place according to the three tiers of instructional support: Benchmark, Strategic, and Intensive. Assessments used must demonstrate reliability and validity and be easy and efficient to administer, score, and interpret (see earlier discussion of using existing assessments to help serve this purpose).

Another way to think of benchmark testing is to consider it a prediction of the future. Students falling in the Intensive category who do not receive interventions are unlikely to be successful in the future. For reading and math, the consequences are dire. Students in the Intensive range are unlikely to pass state-level efficiency exams and unlikely to be successful in grade-level coursework.

Screening is designed as part of a schoolwide approach to intervention. It will help you identify

- how many students need additional instructional support,
- which students need additional instructional support, and
- what level of instructional support is required.

When Conducting Benchmark Testing: Considerations for Implementation

- Identify if existing data are available via state testing results, MAP, and so on. If not, what assessment system will be used?
- Identify an assessment plan for efficiently completing benchmark testing. Ideally, an assessment team is used to complete testing within a short time span (1 week).
- Additional benchmarking (winter and spring) can be used to evaluate effectiveness of interventions/systems.
- Benchmark tests should be conducted with all students at their grade level. The results are intended to illustrate where students are relative to grade-level expectations.

> Consider . . . Strive to complete benchmark testing as soon as possible at the beginning of the school year so the results can be used for arranging class schedules for the fall. Many schools establish intervention groups and classes for the fall based on spring screening results. Of course, after the start of school adjustments can be made, but waiting until fall to organize intervention groups is too late.

Step 2.

What: Define and validate the need for support.

How: Use results from (A) benchmark testing to identify the overall level of instructional support necessary and (B) diagnostic assessments to define and identify specific skills to be taught.

A. Benchmark Testing and the
Three-Tiered Instructional Support Approach:

- Instructional recommendation categories:
  - *Benchmark:* Established skill performance across all administered measures.
  - *Strategic:* One or more skill areas are not within the expected performance range.
  - *Intensive:* One or more skill areas are significantly below the expected performance range.

Classifying Instructional Needs Using Percentiles

Content Area	Measure	Critical Value
		40 percentile and above = Benchmark
Math	CBM	39–20 percentile = Strategic
Reading	Maze, Cloze	
Written Expression	CBM	Below 20 percentile = Intensive
Spelling	CBM	
Content Area Learning	CBM	

- Instructional recommendations are based on performance across all measures.
- Instructional recommendations provide a general description of the instructional intensity needed for improvement.

Students identified as meeting Benchmark are skill proficient and likely to be successful in content area classes.

Students identified as Strategic will likely need targeted intervention to address specific skill deficits, such as reading comprehension, grammar, composition, and so on.

Students identified Intensive typically need an instructional program that is explicit, systematic, and highly structured (consider using a comprehensive reading and math program to support Intensive students).

YOUR TURN

Take a moment to

1. Reflect on the assessments used in your building,

2. Identify what academic skills are being assessed,

3. Assess to what degree do your existing assessments allow instructional decision making?

4. Evaluate whether assessments are

   o time efficient and easily administered,

- o used for identifying students in need of instructional supports according to a three-tier model,
- o valid and reliable measures,
- o capable of a basic level of error analysis,
- o also validated for progress monitoring, and
- o easily understood and utilized by teachers.

B. Use Diagnostic Assessment to Define and Target Instructional Skills

Diagnostic Assessment

Purpose of Assessment	Definition
Screening	Used to identify students in need of instructional support
Diagnostic←	**Used to provide more in-depth analysis of a student's strengths and weaknesses to guide instruction**
Progress Monitoring	Used to ensure that a student is on track and for making course corrections
Outcome	End of year benchmark testing used to determine what percent of students at a particular grade met grade-level outcomes

Diagnostic assessment follows screening and is administered when additional information is necessary to clarify or pinpoint specific skill deficits. Diagnostic assessment provides more detailed information about skill development and helps teachers plan instruction and determine which specific interventions are needed.

Diagnostic assessments are commonly used with Strategic and low Benchmark students to help pinpoint specific skills to be targeted by supplemental instruction. For students in these two categories, targeting specific skill deficits can be effective since not everything needs to be taught.

Intensive students, on the other hand, might be administered in-program placement tests that specify where students enter an intervention program rather than assessed using multiple diagnostic assessments. Placement tests serve as the diagnostic test for Intensive students. In short, placement tests inform (1) student placement in the program and (2) grouping of students (i.e., students with like placements are grouped together).

Consider... Intensive students often have learning characteristics that make targeting specific and isolated skills a difficult undertaking. Rather, intensive students are often more likely to be successful in a systematic and highly structured comprehensive intervention program such as Language! published by Voyager Sopris Learning. With this approach rather than targeting missing skills, learning is sequential, comprehensive, and preventative.

Below are the recommended steps for conducting diagnostic assessment. Begin by reviewing the error analysis from Benchmark testing. Then, use informal diagnostic measures, referred to as *functional academic assessments* (FAAs).

First, conduct skills analysis for Benchmark and Strategic students identified as in need of instructional support. Begin by reviewing their probes to determine current skills and patterns of performance. For instance, is their reading accurate but low fluency, or is there a high error rate?

Second, utilize FAAs.

Functional academic assessments are informal, brief diagnostic assessments used to evaluate specific academic skills. Since they are informal and used for the purpose of informing instruction rather than eligibility, they typically *do not* require parental consent.

FAA Examples

- Phonics/Decoding Screening Test
- CORE (Consortium On Reading Excellence) Assessing Reading: Multiple Measures
- Ekwall/Shanker Reading Inventory
- EasyCBM Error Analysis
- Curriculum-Based Evaluation (CBE)
- Program Assessments (placement tests)

FAAs are particularly useful for identifying specific skill deficits and error patterns. Consider the following example:

What if comprehension is low?

Ask why. Does the student

- devote too much attention to figuring out words?
- make word-reading errors and lose the sense of the passage while struggling?
- alter attention to determine the meaning of individual words?
- take so long getting to the end of the passage that he or she can't remember the beginning of the passage?
- have poor or underdeveloped vocabulary skills?
- lack comprehension strategies (i.e., read as if everything were equally unimportant)?

Step 3.

> **What:** Explore and plan instructional interventions to meet student needs.
>
> **How:** Align intervention/instructional supports to identified instructional needs (i.e., group students accordingly). See the Assessment/Instruction Chart, page 93.

Step 4.

> **What:** Look and review results to ensure instructional supports are effective.
>
> **How:** Use progress monitoring to inform instructional decisions as well as to ensure students are on track for achieving outcome goals.

Progress Monitoring

Purpose of Assessment	Method of Assessment	Definition
Screening	Benchmark Testing	Used to identify students in need of instructional support

(Continued)

(Continued)

Purpose of Assessment	Method of Assessment	Definition
Diagnostic	Functional Assessment	Used to provide more in-depth information of a student's skill deficits
Progress Monitoring←	**CBM/In-program Assessment**	**Used to monitor a student's progression of achievement and to allow adjustments to instructional techniques**
Outcome		End-of-year benchmark testing used to determine what percentage of students at a particular grade met grade-level outcomes

Whereas screening assessment can give a glimpse into a student's future by assessing current performance and predicting probability for academic success, intervention is the means to alter that prediction. To evaluate the effectiveness of the intervention, that students are learning, and to ensure newly taught skills are generalized, progress monitoring is applied. There are two types of progress monitoring:

Type of Progress Monitoring	Information Provided
1. In-program or instructional assessment	Are students learning content?
2. Out-of-program assessment (CBMs)	Are students generalizing—can they apply the skills in a different context?

In-Program Progress Monitoring

In-program monitoring requires evaluating how much content is being covered (pacing) as well as how well students are mastering instructional concepts. In-program or instructional monitoring is arguably the most important because it provides information necessary for adjusting daily instruction. Frequently, when students fail to make sufficient progress, it is due to the fact that not enough content is being covered to allow students to make catch-up growth, they are not actually learning the content being covered, or both. In-program monitoring will be discussed in-depth in Chapter 5.

Out-of-Program Progress Monitoring

Out-of-program progress monitoring provides information regarding a student's generalization and ability to apply skills previously taught. Struggling students often "have it" today but don't "have it" tomorrow or can apply a skill in one context but fail to generalize to others. For this reason, out-of-program progress monitoring is critical. It is important to keep in mind that students cannot generalize what they are not learning. For this reason, in-program or instructional monitoring is critical.

Important Considerations for Progress Monitoring

How often should we progress monitor at the secondary level?

National Center on Student Progress Monitoring

SCHEDULE FOR PROGRESS MONITORING			
Type of Monitoring	*Benchmark*	*Strategic*	*Intensive*
In-program monitoring instruction	As indicated by core program (for example, theme, skill tests, and so on)	On-going to assess obtainment of targeted skills	As indicated by intervention program (for example, check out mastery assessments, and so on)
Out-of-program (CBMs)		Every 3 to 4 weeks	Twice per month

What are examples of the out-of-program measures?

Out-of-Program Progress-Monitoring Measures

Area	*Measure*
Reading	EasyCBM (reading)
Reading Comprehension	CBM (Maze, Cloze)

(Continued)

(Continued)

Area	Measure
Math	CBM (computation, concepts, application, number sense)
Written Expression	CBM (TWW, CWS, WSC)
Content Area Learning	CBM (vocabulary matching)

Remember—CBMs are excellent for out-of-program progress monitoring, because they

- are reliable and valid,
- are easy to administer and score,
- measure generalization,
- promote decision making, and
- can be graphed.

What are the steps for progress monitoring?
When progress monitoring, the following steps apply:

1. Students' current levels of performance are determined, and goals are identified to ensure ambitious and realistic expectations for growth.

2. Students' academic performance is measured on a regular basis.

3. Students' progression is monitored, and instruction is adjusted to meet group and individual learning needs.

First, monitoring academic goals begin with consideration for the group or individual's present level of performance and a timeline. The present level of performance or baseline is most often based on the student's or group's instructional level. This rather than grade placement is their present level of performance and is the level from which a goal is based.

Next, Identify a Goal and Timeline

As goals are established, it is necessary to keep several concerns in mind:

1. What is the outcome goal?

What proficiency level is required for success?

2. What is the instructional group or student's current level of skill?

3. How much growth is needed?

4. How much growth does this require per week?

For example, to set a goal for reading fluency

1. identify starting words correct per minute (wcpm) (for example, 60 wcpm),

2. identify end of semester grade-level target (for example, 120 wcpm),

3. subtract current wcpm from target and determine the amount of growth required,

4. identify the typical growth for students of the same instructional level and establish a goal that allows the student to make sufficient progress toward accelerated growth,

5. divide the expected weekly growth by the total amount of growth required and establish a timeline for achieving the goal. Is the rate of growth ambitious and realistic? Does it allow the student to be at grade level by the end of the semester, or will additional time be required?

6. using a two week or monthly growth expectation, assess student progress accordingly, and

7. continue to monitor and make changes as indicated according to decision rules. See decision rules on page 104. Ensure progress of the entire instructional group using Kidgraph.

Goals can be established for instructional groups or individual students. The goal is the intended outcome.
Goals must be

1. Ambitious: Take into consideration how much growth is necessary for students to catch up or maintain parallel growth (once at grade level). If not ambitious, students will fail to progress at a level necessary to close the achievement gap.

2. Realistic: Goals should target obtainable levels of academic growth. Unrealistic growth expectations will result in faulty decision making as students fail to live up to the unrealistic expectations. If goals are too high, one could conclude that students are not responding to intervention and unnecessarily change interventions. See Hasbrouck and Tindal (2005), below:

Jan Hasbrouck and Gerald Tindal have completed an extensive study of oral reading fluency. The results of their study were published in a technical report titled "Oral Reading Fluency: 90 Years of Measurement," which is available on the following website, www.brtprojects.org/publications/dl/51, and in *The Reading Teacher* in 2006.

The table below shows the mean oral reading fluency of students in Grades 1 through 8 as determined by Hasbrouck and Tindal's data.

You can use the information in this table to draw conclusions and make decisions about the oral reading fluency of your students. **Students scoring 10 or more words below the 50th percentile using the average score of two unpracticed readings from grade-level materials need a fluency building program.** In addition, teachers can use the table to set the long-term fluency goals for their struggling readers.

Average weekly improvement is the average words per week growth you can expect from a student. It was calculated by subtracting the fall score from the spring score and dividing the difference by 32, the typical number of weeks between the fall and spring assessments.

Grade	Percentile	Fall WCPM*	Winter WCPM*	Spring WCPM*	Avg. Weekly Improvement**
1	90	–	81	111	1.9
	75	–	47	82	2.2
	50	–	23	53	1.9
	25	–	12	28	1.0
	10	–	6	15	0.6
2	90	106	125	142	1.1
	75	79	100	117	1.2
	50	51	72	89	1.2
	25	25	42	61	1.1
	10	11	18	31	0.6
3	90	128	146	162	1.1
	75	99	120	137	1.2
	50	71	92	107	1.1
	25	44	62	78	1.1
	10	21	36	48	0.8
4	90	145	166	180	1.1
	75	119	139	152	1.0

Grade	Percentile	Fall WCPM*	Winter WCPM*	Spring WCPM*	Avg. Weekly Improvement**
	50	94	112	123	0.9
	25	68	87	98	0.9
	10	45	61	72	0.8
5	90	166	182	194	0.9
	75	139	156	168	0.9
	50	110	127	139	0.9
	25	85	99	109	0.8
	10	61	74	83	0.7
6	90	177	195	204	0.8
	75	153	167	177	0.8
	50	127	140	150	0.7
	25	98	111	122	0.8
	10	68	82	93	0.8
7	90	180	192	202	0.7
	75	156	165	177	0.7
	50	128	136	150	0.7
	25	102	109	123	0.7
	10	79	88	98	0.6
8	90	185	199	199	0.4
	75	161	173	177	0.5
	50	133	146	151	0.6
	25	106	115	124	0.6
	10	77	84	97	0.6

Source: Copyright © 2005. Behavioral Research and Teaching. All rights reserved. This publication, or parts thereof, may not be used or reproduced in any manner without written permission.

*WCPM = Words Correct Per Minute

**Average weekly improvement is the average words per week growth you can expect from a student.

How Much Growth Is Required?

Identify the amount of growth required to close the gap and then determine a realistic timeline.

EXAMPLE: MARY

Mary: 7th Grade (January)

- What is the outcome goal?

  The spring benchmark for 7th grade ORF is a minimum of 136 correct words per minute.

- What is the present level of performance?

  10 wpm, 3rd Grade DIBELS ORF

- How much growth is needed?

  30 wpm by the spring benchmark

- How much growth does this require per week?

  30 divided by 16 weeks = 2 words per week

- In this example, progress monitor using grade-level material.

EXAMPLE: JILL

Jill: 9th Grade (January)
Area: Math

- What is the outcome goal?

  The spring benchmark for 6th grade CBM Math is a minimum of 140 correct digits (cds).

- What is the present level of performance (PLOP)?

  38 cds, 4th Grade

- How much growth is needed?

  15 cds by the spring benchmark

- How much growth does this require per week?

  15 divided by 18 weeks = .83 cds per week

EXAMPLE: BUNKY

Bunky: 8th Grade

- Reading Level = 65 wpm, 6th Grade
- Benchmark for 8th Grade = 146 wpm
- Necessary Gain (wpm) = 66

  9 wks =   8.8
  18 wks =   4.4
  27 wks =   2.96

- Minimum of an 18 Week Goal: 4.4 wpm per week
- In 18 weeks, on 2nd grade DIBELS probes, Bunky will read 90 words per minute.

YOUR TURN

DATA-BASED DECISION MAKING—ACTIVITY 4

Set a Reading Goal for Dan

Identify the amount of growth required to close the gap and create a realistic timeline.

Dan: 6th Grade

- Reading Level = 68 wpm, 4th Grade
- Benchmark for 3rd Grade = 127 wpm
- Necessary Gain (wpm) = 59 wpm

  9 wks =
  18 wks =
  27 wks =

- Use the average growth chart to help establish an ambitious but realistic time frame and expected weekly growth.

How Are Decisions Made? Apply Graphing Conventions

Benefits of Graphing

- A graph is often the best way to show data because it is often easier to interpret data in this form. It creates a picture of learning to document results.
- A graph motivates students.
- It helps teachers make decisions and predict outcomes.

Graphing Terminology

Baseline: the point used for comparison; the student's performance before intervention.

Aimline: the line on a graph that shows the expected rate of change—the expected rate of learning.

Trend line: the line on a graph that shows the general direction in which something is headed—the student's current performance.

Phase line: the vertical line that indicates a change was made—a change in intervention (that is, double dose, and so on).

Example: Basic Monitoring Graph

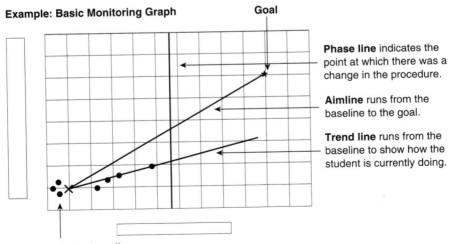

Example: Basic Monitoring Graph

Goal

Phase line indicates the point at which there was a change in the procedure.

Aimline runs from the baseline to the goal.

Trend line runs from the baseline to show how the student is currently doing.

X represents the **baseline:** typical performance before intervention.

Graphing Conventions

- Plot the junction of the day and the data on one dot.
- Usually connect all data points, unless there is break of longer than one week.
- Record absences in data boxes.
- Mark vacations with double vertical lines.
- Place a double hash mark at the zero point if not counting up from zero.

Baseline data should be

- stable:
  - three measures or more,
  - collected in the appropriate setting(s), and
  - collected in a relatively short period of time; and

- representative:
  - teacher says it is "typical";
  - data accurately describe behavior as it naturally occurs.

The aimline

- shows the expected or predicted rate of learning from the baseline to the goal,
- shows the course to follow to reach the goal, and
- allows ongoing decision making regarding progress toward the goal.

Example: Aimline

Goal for Cayley: In 18 weeks, when presented with random fifth-grade reading passages, Cayley will read aloud at a rate of 73 wpm for three of five trials.

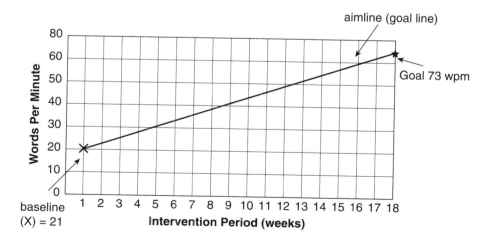

Apply Data Decision Rules

What is a data decision rule? It is a procedure by which patterns of progress-monitoring data are analyzed over time. Data analysis helps educators make decisions about student learning and the effectiveness of instruction.

Why Are There Data Decision Rules?

- So you know whether to continue or modify an intervention
- Because you don't have unlimited time to continue with interventions that are not working
- To guide instructional decisions
- So you can see which things work and which things don't work for your students

What Rules Can I Use for Making Decisions?

Moving Median: The decision is made when three consecutive data points fall above or below the aimline.

What Is a Moving Median, and How Do I Graph It?

- A moving median is a quick and easy method to reduce variability, and it eliminates the need for a trend line.
- A moving median is a method for graphing the median of the three newest scores.

1. Draw the aimline.

2. Administer one probe each week for three weeks and record the raw data on the graph.

3. After three weeks, use the three data points to make a decision according to data decision rules.

4. Each week thereafter, plot the median of your three newest scores (most recent plus two previous).

Moving Median Data Decision Rules

1. If three consecutive data points are above the aimline, consider raising the criteria. Was the goal ambitious enough? Could it be increased?

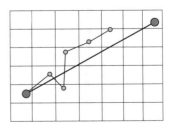

2. If three consecutive data points are below the aimline, consider changes to the intervention—see alterable variables in Chapter 5.

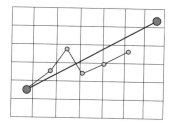

3. If the data points align with the aim line, the group or student is making adequate progress toward the established goal, maintain.

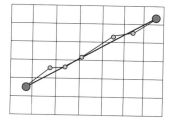

YOUR TURN

DATA-BASED DECISION MAKING—ACTIVITY 5

1. Look at the first chart.

2. Should you continue on the same course or make changes?

3. Using the Alterable Variables Chart below, identify possible changes to improve student academic progress.

Apply Decision-Making Rules

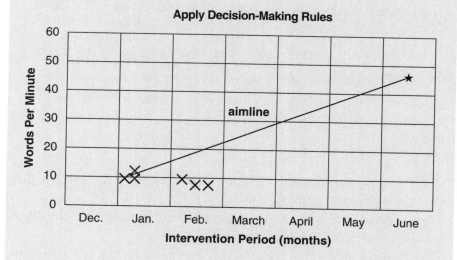

(Continued)

(Continued)

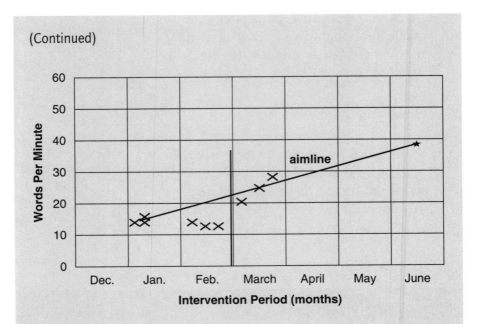

What does the above line mean? Referring to the four questions below as well as the Alterable Variables Chart, identify possible considerations for improving the student's response to instruction.

When evaluating the effectiveness of intervention, consider these four questions:

1. Are we teaching the right thing (targeting the right skills, using the most effective method/program)?

2. Are we teaching enough of it to allow the students to catch up (pacing)?

3. Are students learning what is being taught (in-program assessment)?

4. Are students generalizing skills (out-of-program assessment)?

Considerations Regarding Decision Making

- Focus on the question: "Will the individual reach his or her goal by the end of the goal period?"
- Consider making a change to the intervention whenever the rate of progress falls below the expectation.
- Think of changes to the intervention as fine tuning (alterable variables) rather than as major reconstruction of interventions.

Alterable Variables Chart

Alterable Components	Specific Adjustments				
Opportunities to Learn (Time and/or Concentration of Instruction)	Increase attendance.	Provide instruction daily.	Increase opportunities to respond.	Vary schedule of easy and difficult tasks and skills.	Add another instructional period.
Program Efficacy	Preteach components of core program.	Use extension of core program.	Supplement core with appropriate materials.	Replace current core program.	Implement specially designed program.
Program Implementation	Model lesson delivery.	Monitor implementation frequently.	Provide coaching and ongoing support.	Provide additional staff development.	Vary program and/or lesson schedule.
Grouping for Instruction	Check group placement.	Reduce group size.	Increase teacher-led instruction.	Provide individual instruction.	Change instructor.
Coordination of Instruction	Clarify instructional priorities.	Establish concurrent reading periods.	Provide complementary reading instruction across periods.	Establish communication across instructors.	Meet frequently to examine progress.

Source: Robinson, J. (2009, March). Oregon Reading First: Cohort B Leadership Session, Center on Teaching and Learning (CTL), University of Oregon. Portland, OR. Used with permission.

Considerations When Modifying an Intervention

When decision rules indicate that it's time to make a change, consider alterable variables before changing to another intervention.

Consider...Progress monitoring helps evaluate the effectiveness of instruction and allows adjustments to ensure students are successful. Both in-program and out-of-program progress monitoring is essential, especially for struggling learners. Some of the benefits of progress monitoring include the following:

- Maximized instructional effectiveness
- Improved learning outcomes for students
- Improved communication among teachers, parents or guardians, and students regarding student progress
- Improved systems effectiveness
- Accelerated learning because instructional adjustments can be made as soon as a problem is identified
- Instructional decisions are objective
- Increased student motivation

Graphing Practice

Student's Name <u>Cynthia</u>   Dist/Bldg. ————   Grade <u>7</u>   Teacher ————

Baseline ————   Goal <u>In 9 weeks, when presented 7th grade mixed math probes, Cynthia will write 20 correct digits per 2 minute probe, in 3 out of 5 trials.</u>

Evaluation Procedure ————————————————————

Title(s) of Person(s) Responsible for Services ———————————————

Milestones   Objective 1 ————————   Objective 2 ————————

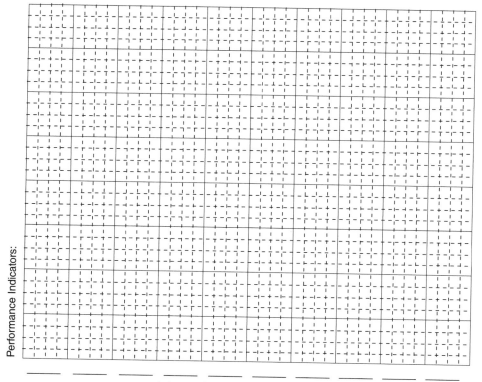

Baseline in first column

Performance Indicators:

Intervention Period (months)

Instructions: Complete this progress-monitoring graph for Cynthia. Include

    a. The baseline present level of performance

    b. The goal aimline

    c. Plot the data points on the graph using the data corresponding to Weeks 1 through 4 at the bottom of the graph.

    d. Apply the moving-median decision rules after completing Cynthia's progress-monitoring graph. Should the intervention plan be continued or changed?

M				9	14					
T	8	10		11						
W	10	11	13	10						
Th	11									
F										

COMPONENT FOUR: A COMMUNICATION PLAN FOR DATA ANALYSES AND INSTRUCTIONAL DECISION MAKING

> **How:** Conducting data meetings and using powerful ways of displaying data.

Without a well-thought-out plan to analyze and communicate obtained data, all the hard work of the proceeding steps will likely be wasted. To avoid this potential pitfall, schools must develop a format for displaying, interpreting, and using the obtained data. Such a format should ensure intervention teachers are directly involved, otherwise buy-in and ownership will most certainly be problematic.

For instance, consider the difference in how you respond to two scenarios: (1) someone informs you that what you are doing is not working versus (2) through experience and directly reviewing results, you identify for yourself that something is not working. Being told by someone else results in defensive mechanisms that interfere with accepting facts and making necessary changes. Actively collecting and interpreting data in a structured format with colleagues leads to more active problem solving, improved systems, and improved student outcomes.

Steps for developing a communication plan for data analyses and instructional decision making include (1) holding departmental and building-level data meetings, and (2) using visual displays for interpreting data.

Departmental meetings should occur a minimum of once per month. Topics might include

- Review Progress-Monitoring Data, In-program assessments, and Lesson Progress Reports for all instructional groups (B, S, I)
- Identify Instructional Modifications for Groups not making adequate progress (e.g., identified an instructional group requiring increased content pacing)
- Identify Instructional Modifications for Individuals (e.g., identify particular students within a group requiring a preteach and reteach of daily lessons)

- Professional Development: (e.g., watched an Anita Acher video demonstrating maximizing opportunities for students to respond)

The purpose of departmental data meetings is to review grade-level data; identify systems, groups, and individual students who need support; and then plan required support.

Building-level meetings should occur at least three times per year in which all staff are involved in reviewing and analyzing data. A building-level meeting might include (1) reviewing schoolwide data, (2) reviewing departmental team outcomes and suggested actions, (3) identifying a schoolwide action plan, and (4) developing a list of necessary resources and professional development for the school.

Implementation Checklist

1. A comprehensive measurements system that addresses the multiple purposes of assessment

   - School assessments fulfill the four purposes of assessment in reading and math
   - Assessment used meets the criteria of "good assessment"
     - o Facilitates instructional decision making
     - o Easily administered, scored, and interpreted
     - o Measures skills that are important and predictive of academic success
     - o Fits within day-to-day instructional routines
     - o Valid and reliable

2. A data management system that summarizes the data in easy-to-interpret reports

   - Data are summarized in easy-to-read and easy-to-interpret reports.
   - Teachers have received training in how to read and use data reports.
   - Report formats are understood and used by all teachers.

3. A formative decision-making model

   - Screening is used to identify students in need of instructional supports in reading and math.
   - Goals for expected performance are clearly identified for each benchmark testing period and for each grade.

- Screening results provide recommendations and placement in relation to the three levels of instructional support.
- Diagnostic testing is informal and used to guide decisions regarding skills to be taught.
- Intervention placement tests are used for students requiring Intensive supports.
- Student performance profiles are used to determine instructional focus.
- In-program monitoring is used to evaluate pacing and student learning of instructional content.
- Out-of-program monitoring is used to evaluate student generalization of skills as well as evaluate progress toward outcome goals.
- Staff members are trained how to read and make decisions using progress-monitoring data.

4. A communication plan for data analyses and instructional decision making

- The school has regular (at least monthly), structured grade-level data meetings.
- The school holds schoolwide data meetings in which grade-level data are shared and discussed.
- The school uses powerful visual formats to display, communicate, and facilitate interpretation of data.

5. Create a Schoolwide Assessment Plan using the format provided below. Be sure to clearly address the following:

Data-Based Decision Making

1. For each area, consider the purposes and types of assessment needed. Identify members of your school's assessment team. Decide who will do which assessments.

2. What schedule of progress monitoring will be applied for Benchmark, Strategic, and Intensive students? What assessments will be administered?

3. Identify a format to ensure that progress monitoring is systematically used for instructional decision making. How will the results be shared and used?

	Purpose of Assessment	What Assessment Will Be Used	How Often Will It Be Administered	Who Will Administer	How Will Results Be Shared or Displayed
R	SCREENING				
E	Benchmark Students				
A	Strategic Students				
D	Intensive Students				
I	DIAGNOSTIC				
N	Benchmark Students				
G	Strategic Students				
	Intensive Students				
	PROGRESS MONITORING				
	Benchmark Students				
	Strategic Students				
	Intensive Students				
M	SCREENING				
A	Benchmark Students				
T	Strategic Students				
H					

CONCLUSION

Even the best research-validated interventions will not work equally well for everyone and will not work if not implemented with fidelity. The only way to truly guard against intervention failures is to closely monitor student progress using assessments designed to be sensitive to changes in skill sets. This chapter outlined a comprehensive plan for using assessments to inform instruction as part of a schoolwide approach to RTI. Using existing data (MAP, ACT, etc.), curriculum-based assessments, program-specific assessments, and functional academic assessments (diagnostic) were presented along with an overall framework organizing and using the resulting data. Secondary schools armed with a strong assessment plan dramatically improve their odds of establishing RTI systems that are and remain effective. Indeed, students with skills deficits deserve no less. Ensuring that what we do is effective is a professional and moral obligation of our profession.

Blank worksheets and user forms discussed in this chapter are available for download at **www.partnersforlearning.org**.

Establishing Effective Teams

5

This chapter cowritten by Amy Ruane

OBJECTIVES:

- To identify characteristics of effective teams
- To learn how to run effective meetings
- To learn how to make effective decisions

TEAMS WORK BETTER WHEN THEY WORK TOGETHER

Mrs. Clawson is a seventh-grade English teacher at Ustick Middle School. Despite having concerns about several students in her second and fourth period classes, she is reluctant to make a referral to the school's Care Team. Previous experiences have been frustrating. In her words "nothing is ever accomplished . . . we talk and talk, but students rarely ever are helped as a result of our meetings." If you have been in education long, you have undoubtedly served or participated on a school-based team responsible for addressing struggling students. Your experiences may have ranged from a positive, productive meeting to one long and drawn-out where little more than "admiring the problem" was accomplished. Educators complain, and rightly so, of lengthy meetings that serve little more than to document that procedural protocols were followed. For many teachers, this is a source of great frustration; for education, this is a sign such processes need to be reevaluated and in many instances re-designed.

Major considerations involved in effective teaming include (a) identifying the purpose of the team, (b) understanding the nature of effective teams, (c) establishing strong leadership, (d) understanding elements of successful meetings, (e) specifying meeting rules and/or responsibilities, (f) public recording, (g) establishing a collaborative environment, and (h) a process for decision making.

IDENTIFYING THE PURPOSE OF THE TEAM

Grade/Departmental-Level Meetings

For the promise of RTI to be realized in a meaningful way, it is necessary that regular education teachers maintain primary ownership of the process and establish routines to support the core instructional practices associated with RTI. This requires grade/departmental-level teachers have the opportunity and responsibility for evaluating their effectiveness of their systems as well as having a process for addressing identified concerns. For this to happen, grade/departmental-level teachers must have the opportunity to meet together on a regular basis and be trained how to have effective data meetings.

Grade/departmental-level meetings are composed of grade/departmental-level teachers, the principal, and specialists, as necessary. The meetings include the following activities:

- review grade/departmental-level data,
- update data boards and evaluate group and individual student progress,
- review effectiveness of system-level supports,
- problem solve systems in need of improvement,
- problem solve instructional groups and individual students,
- create action plans for addressing identified concerns, and
- plan and collaborate other grade/departmental-level topics.

BUILDING-LEVEL RTI TEAMS

Whereas grade/departmental-level teams are responsible for planning, evaluating, and problem solving grade/departmental-level systems and students, building-level teams are responsible for conducting schoolwide evaluation and problem solving. Building-level RTI teams provide ongoing oversight to grade/departmental-level teams, ensure coordination across grades, and assist specific grade/departmental-level teams when asked or directed to do so.

Building-level teams are composed of grade/departmental-level representatives, the principal, and various specialists. Responsibilities include

- review schoolwide data,
- review effectiveness of schoolwide supports,
- problem solve system-level concerns across or within particular grades,
- review grade/departmental-level outcomes,
- problem solve issues referred by grade/departmental level teams,
- problem solve and develop an intervention for individual students referred by grade/departmental-level teams, and
- track Intervention Plans (I-Plans)—conduct comprehensive evaluations as necessary.

Effective Teams

To establish and maintain a productive school-based team is difficult. To be sustained long term, the team will require strong leadership, persistence, and strategic planning. Regardless of the team's purpose, effective teams more often have clear unity of purpose and clearly defined group process. They have high expectations and are seldom sidetracked or fail to live up to their identified performance goals. Despite their "all business" mentality, the atmosphere around the team is typically informal, comfortable, and relaxed. All members of the team contribute and share the common goal of improved educational outcomes.

Above all, effective teams contain the following three elements

1. Leadership

Effective teams have effective leaders. Effective team leaders

- Generate a democratic framework
- Do not rely on established formulas for getting things done; they set the example of a "whatever it takes" mentality
- Model problem solving; they support and encourage others to identify needs and develop solutions
- Know that better learning environments are created by high expectations and educators with a strong knowledge base working in a supportive system

2. Flexibility

Productive teams are flexible in their approach to the task at hand. Strong teams, like strong leaders, also have a "whatever it takes" mentality as a core value. Team members are selected on the basis of their potential contribution to the team and team process as a whole.

3. Energy

A major source of a team's energy is derived from their sense of purpose and drive. For such teams, problems are viewed as obstacles and resources are manipulated to achieve end results. For such teams

- Meetings are efficient and purpose driven
- Feelings and ideas are freely expressed
- Disagreement is present and viewed as good
- Decisions are made with general agreement
- Team members share responsibility and follow group norms
- Constructive evaluation occurs frequently
- Group leadership shifts from time to time
- The work completed is viewed as meaningful and effective

EFFECTIVE MEETINGS

The art of running effective meetings is arranging and finessing the elements that make up productive meetings. The elements include

1. Clear and meaningful objectives—meetings serve a specific purpose; they are not held to complete paperwork. Rather, team members expect data to be shared, problems to be identified and defined, and a clear plan of action to be created.

2. Identifying and enforcing group norms—team members operate according to agreed upon rules of conduct.

3. Clarifying what members need to do or bring in preparation for the meeting—members come to each meeting prepared with necessary data that has been collected and summarized.

4. Ensuring decisions are acted upon through development of action plans—such plans specify what is to be carried out, by whom, and when. They also include a means to measure the results of the action to be completed.

5. Meeting notes are recorded and reviewed at subsequent meetings.

Establishing Meeting Roles

Engaged Participants

- actively seek and provide data relevant to the problem,
- are open to the ideas and feelings of others,
- allow others to speak and use effective listening skills to understand what is being said, and
- contribute to the team process and support a goal-oriented atmosphere.

The Facilitator

- keeps the group on task and directs the process,
- encourages active participation from all members,
- clarifies ideas and protects ideas from attack, and
- redirects the process as necessary to prevent the team from becoming sidetracked.

The Recorder

- records basic ideas,
- clarifies with groups what should and should not be recorded, and
- maintains record of meetings and shares with other interested parties.

Person With Role or Knowledge Authority

- provides information to the group about constraints and resources,
- is an active participant,
- ensures that meeting follow-through occurs, and
- is able to commit building resources, make administrative decisions.

Public Recording

Recording the meeting in a public manner, such as on a whiteboard, a computer, or a flip chart serves several purposes. It

1. Focuses the group on the task.

2. Supports visual learners.

3. Depersonalizes ideas and problem-bearing data.

4. Prevents repetition.

5. Encourages participation because it respects individual ideas.

6. Ensures ideas are being recorded accurately.

7. Allows for information developed in one phase of the problem solving to be used in the next.

8. Makes accountability easier because decisions are written down in clear view of the group: who is doing what, when. (Garmston & Wellman, 2002)

Collaborative Meetings

The ultimate success of a team meeting depends on the cooperation and collaboration of its team members. Collaborative meetings, therefore, require a format that ensures conversations are focused and intentions and purposes are clearly defined. As mentioned earlier, organizing meetings around student data offers teams the advantage of objectively identifying problems (systems and students), identifying reasons for the concerns, and focusing on possible solutions. A well-defined problem-solving format is also a key ingredient.

THE PROBLEM-SOLVING PROCESS

Garmston and Wellman (2002) described a decision-making process that includes four problem-solving steps.

Step 1. Brainstorm

Elicit ideas only and push for between six to eight ideas. Record the brainstormed ideas on chart paper for everyone to see. Discourage criticisms or questions during the brainstorming phase. Criticism or evaluative statements create the feeling of an unsafe environment and undermine the power of the brainstorming process.

Step 2. Clarify

Ask whether any ideas need clarification and let the author of the question provide the clarification. Be careful to limit the conversation to explaining ideas rather than evaluating their merit or trying to work out logistical details. Example of clarifying: "John, when you suggested a double dose, how much additional instructional time did you have in mind?" Non-example: "John, when you suggested a double dose, how do you suppose we make that happen with our limited staff?"

Step 3. Advocate

Participants may advocate for as many ideas as they wish and as many times as they wish. Statements of advocacy must be phrased positively, and they must be brief. Remember, advocate for ideas you feel will work—do not evaluate or criticize ideas.

Step 4. Canvass

Ask individuals in the group to identify a few ideas (from two to four) they think are likely to address the identified problems. Ideas may be combined to create a powerful plan. The ideas do not need to be in rank order. Discuss which ideas have the greatest likelihood for resolving the problem and determine which are of greatest interest to the group.

Develop an Action Plan

A purposeful meeting should include the development of an action plan. Such a plan will help ensure ideas and solutions live beyond the meeting. An action plan should identify

- Who will do what, when?
- What will be communicated regarding the decisions of the meeting, and who will communicate the decisions?
- What are the next steps?
- When will you follow up?

Remember: A goal without a plan is just a wish!

TEN CONSIDERATIONS FOR SUCCESSFUL TEAMING

In summary, effective meetings are the result of focused, skilled teams. They require extensive planning, ongoing evaluation, and maintenance to sustain themselves. Ten considerations for a successful problem-solving approach include

1. The team determines a regular place and time to meet.

2. Members of the team and attendance expectations are clearly identified.

3. Roles are assigned to team members, including the following:
   o Recorder
   o Timekeeper
   o Facilitator

4. Establish team norms—expectations for problem-solving meetings. They must

   o be data focused;
   o be task oriented;
   o be system and student focused and problem resolution oriented;
   o stay within a specified meeting time frame;
   o have brainstorming rules;
   o require regular attendance;
   o result in assigned responsibilities regarding interventions, data collection, and so on; and
   o have a process for determining case managers for individual students.

5. What process will the team follow for prioritizing issues to be considered during meetings?

6. What criteria are used to determine when to gather additional information? What procedures will be used?

7. What information and data sources will be used as part of the teaming process?

8. How will the team manage information collected as part of the teaming process?

9. Establish a procedure for review and follow-up for concerns addressed during the teaming process.

10. How will the team determine whether its process is effective? How will the team revise and reenergize itself over time?

CONCLUSION

For an RTI school to work efficiently, secondary schools must develop a team process that is efficient and results focused. Too often educators dread meetings as a result of past experiences where time was spent in unproductive sessions in which little was accomplished. To be effective, schools must establish teams with a clear purpose and with strong leadership. Participants must feel their time and input are valued. This is accomplished by establishing clear expectations and guidelines for how meetings are run, including having clear and meaningful objectives, following group norms, how members prepare for meetings, ensuring action plans are developed and meetings are recorded for later review. Finally, ten considerations for successful teaming were presented to guide problem-solving teams at the secondary level.

YOUR TURN

ESTABLISHING EFFECTIVE TEAMS—ACTIVITY 6

Evaluate at least one grade/departmental-level team and the building-wide RTI team. Use the Ten Considerations outlined in this chapter to establish an effective team process.

Blank worksheets and user forms discussed in this chapter are available for download at **www.partnersforlearning.org**.

Problem Solving to Achieve Effective Outcomes— Systems and Students

6

OBJECTIVES:

- To evaluate systems
- To establish RTI teams and processes
- To identify adequate progress
- To problem solve systems
- To problem solve instructional groups
- To problem solve individuals

At Central High School, the Student Study Team (SST) meets every Monday morning to discuss students who are experiencing academic or behavioral/social difficulties. The school established support and intervention classes for students in need. As a result, students receive interventions in reading and math through a schoolwide RTI structure. The purpose of the SST is to discuss students who, although are receiving intervention, continue to struggle and show inadequate progress. The process used by the team is to review what interventions have been tried, evaluate student progress, and make recommendations for possible remedies or next steps. Most often, and as team members can attest, the meetings focus on the student being referred. Students are most often recommended for a change in intervention classes or to receive a comprehensive evaluation to determine eligibility and need for special education. The assumptions going into the weekly meetings and the results of the meeting are typically the same, namely focusing on rather than considering the system itself.

Central High School illustrates how secondary schools often think about and address struggling students. They often start with the assumption that what the school provides is effective and students who do not respond adequately must have some difficulties or qualities that cause them to not respond. Rarely, do schools critically and objectively evaluate the effectiveness of their intervention systems. In other words, they do not ask "Are our interventions working adequately for the majority of our intensive students? Are they working for most and to the degree expected? If not, why?" Most schools do not typically have a clear definition of what effective interventions should produce regarding student outcomes.

This chapter emphasizes the necessity of evaluating and problem solving at the systems and group level BEFORE moving to individual students. The information on evaluating systems is adapted for secondary schools from Oregon Reading First (ORF). It is designed to help schools evaluate the effectiveness of systems, such as "Does our school's Intensive reading intervention plan/system work for the majority of our Intensive students?" It provides a framework for determining systems effectiveness, which instructional supports and interventions are effective as well as insight into what changes will be required to improve outcomes. When data are used systematically at the secondary level, they can be a critical part of realizing effective and sustainable RTI systems for schools as well as individual students. When systems are highly effective, they work for the majority of students, meaning far fewer students will need to be addressed one student at a time.

YOUR TURN

EVALUATING SYSTEMS

Consider the following questions:

1. What is your school's method for determining the effectiveness of systems?

2. Is there a clear standard for determining effectiveness at the system, grade, group, and individual level? What is the standard?

3. How involved are teachers in evaluating the effectiveness of their grade/departmental-level systems? Ask (1) are virtually all Benchmark/proficient students learning standards and passing classes? (2) Are Strategic students in intervention improving their skills as a result of targeted interventions, and (3) are Intensive students at risk becoming less at risk (changing risk categories as a result of system-level interventions).

PROBLEM SOLVING WITHIN THE RTI FRAMEWORK

An Integrated Approach

The model provided below illustrates how schoolwide systems and individual problem solving can be integrated to create a systematic approach to maximize outcomes for all students.

Schoolwide

1. All students receive high quality, research-based instruction in the classroom.

2. General education system includes universal screening of academics and behavior. Existing assessments such as state testing are used for initial screening.

3. School staff implements research-based interventions via intervention classes to address students with difficulties.

4. Interventions are predetermined and available for anyone in need as part of regular education.

5. School staff uses progress-monitoring data to determine interventions' effectiveness and to make modifications as needed. Problem solving occurs initially at the systems and group level.

Individual Student

6. Benchmark assessments are used to evaluate system effectiveness. Students not improving as anticipated are addressed by a problem-solving team. Interventions are designed for individual student needs.

7. Progress monitoring and use of decision rules are applied to ensure adequate progress of individual students.

8. Students with inadequate progress may need special education support.

Teaming for Effectiveness

Multiple educators engaged in problem solving are better than a single person by himself or herself. Having a group of people focused on evaluating a problem provides tremendous potential for influencing and changing structures that are often beyond any one person's circle of control. This is the opportunity to *influence up* by combining educational teaming and problem solving.

One responsibility of a school's Problem-Solving Team (PST) is to provide oversight regarding the health of the overall system. The PST engages in problem-solving activities to address unhealthy parts of the system as well as problems of individual students. Following are additional strategies for schoolwide teaming:

- Establishing grade/departmental-level committees to ensure the health and fidelity of schoolwide systems. Grade/departmental-level teams are composed primarily of regular education teachers who evaluate the progress of groups before problem solving for individual students. Often math teachers evaluate problem math systems; whereas English teachers are responsible for ELA. For each regular content class, questions such as "Are the majority of students passing? If not, why?" and "How do we address students not passing?" are asked. Likewise, the same is asked of intervention classes.
- Both PST and grade-level/departmental teachers use summative and normative data to identify the degree to which programming is effective for each instructional group (Benchmark, Strategic, and Intensive). Are most students within each group making adequate progress?
  - If no, problem solve for the system and/or instructional groups.
  - If yes, problem solve for individual students not making adequate progress.
- Establish and adhere to Problem-Solving Guidelines and format. (See Ten Considerations for Problem Solving on page 124.)

Team Responsibilities

Although problem-solving teams may have a history of serving a variety of purposeful functions within a school, each team should create a written document of clearly stated responsibilities and purposes. Consider the following responsibilities:

1. Understand effective schools research. Know what makes secondary schools effective.

2. Seek to establish a system that is well conceptualized—identify potential problems and work to make systems smooth and effective.

3. Evaluate the extent to which systems are effective at each grade/ departmental level (Benchmark, Strategic, and Intensive).

4. Identify and address systems that are not highly effective.

5. Examine progress of instructional groups on an ongoing basis (monthly). Are students in core classes passing? Are students in intervention progressing as anticipated?

6. Problem solve systems, instructional groups, and individual students.

EVALUATE AND PROBLEM SOLVE SYSTEMS

The RTI Framework on the next page illustrates the systems approach to problem solving. Differentiated levels of support are established using universal assessments such as state tests, MAP, ACT, and so on (Step 1). Progress monitoring and pre-post benchmark assessments are used for a periodic (fall to winter, winter to spring) and ongoing evaluation of system effectiveness. Are enough or most students at each level of support progressing as anticipated? If yes, problem solving is used to address a few students not making adequate progress (individual problem solving). If not enough or most students at a support level are progressing, problem-solving efforts target systems (Step 2). The goal is to identify instructional variables to alter so that particular system becomes more effective. For instance, if a high percentage of students are failing a particular class, what role does the instructional format play? Is only lecture used? Is instruction differentiated? Finally, acute problem solving is used at the individual student level when necessary (Step 3). Data from Steps 1–3 can be used for eligibility decisions in the rare instances when a secondary student is suspected of a disability (Step 4).

In summary, schools must have a way to evaluate

1. The effectiveness of systems and problem solve at three levels: Benchmark, Strategic, and Intensive

RTI Framework

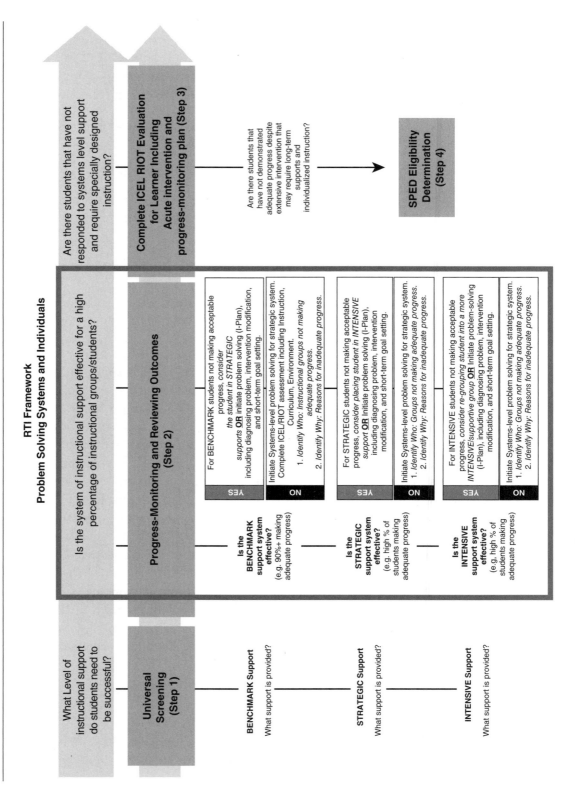

2. The effectiveness of instruction and problem solve at the instructional group levels

3. The progress of individual students and problem solve individuals

What Are the Advantages of Problem Solving for Systems?

- Effective systems improve the performance of all students.
- Most problems are system problems, not student problems.
- Individual problem solving is resource- and time-intensive.
- Individual/student response is linked to effectiveness of systems and progress of groups.
- Ineffective systems decrease the likelihood that individual problem solving will be successful and sustainable.

How Do We Know Whether the System is Effective? Ask:

- Is there something for everyone at each level (Benchmark, Strategic, Intensive)?
- Is it working for most at each of the three levels? Are most students progressing toward becoming or staying proficient?
- Are system-level supports resulting in adequate progress of instructional groups?
- Are system-level supports closing the achievement gap?
- Is there a clear, objective standard to evaluate student growth?

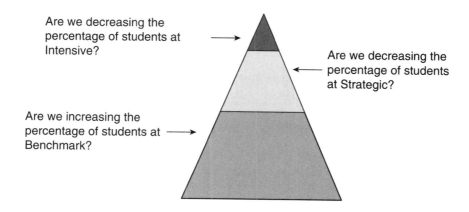

What Percentage of Students Were Benchmark, Strategic, and Intensive in the Fall? Winter?

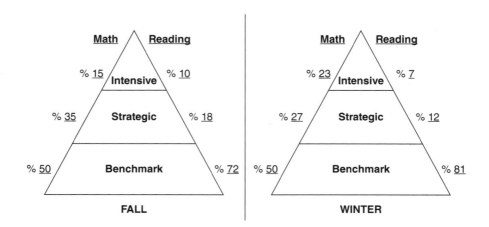

Compare how the percentage of students in each category changed from fall to winter and for both reading and math. Which systems were more effective? Which systems were less effective?

Discussion

In math, the percentage of students proficient in winter and fall is the same. Strategic was decreased by eight percentage points. However, this decrease was due to the students moving to Intensive. In this example, the Strategic math system is not effective. In contrast, the reading system of supports are decreasing students in the Intensive and Strategic ranges while increasing the percentage of students at Benchmark—72 percent in fall to 81 percent in winter. This is an example of an effective system of supports.

YOUR TURN

EFFECTIVE PROBLEM SOLVING: SYSTEMS

Using the forms that follow, evaluate progress from fall to winter and winter to spring.

1. How does the percentage of students in each category compare from fall to winter and winter to spring?

2. Was the school more effective in the first semester or the second?

3. What conclusions can you draw from comparing the fall, winter, and spring data? What questions remain unanswered?

Example Forms—Evaluating Growth

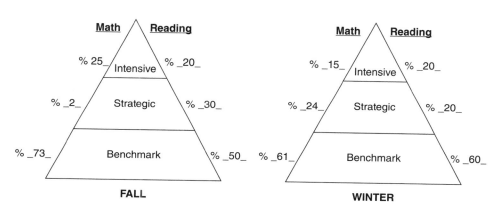

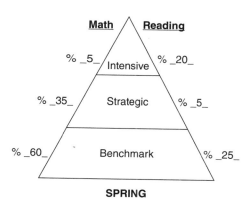

The following table is another useful format for comparing change in benchmark and intensive categories from one benchmark testing period to the next.

	Benchmark Period Fall 2012	Benchmark Period Winter 2013	Percentage Increase or Decrease (+ −)	Intensive Period Fall 2012	Intensive Period Winter 2013	Percentage Increase or Decrease (+ −)
6th Grade	65%	95%	+30%	20%	2%	−18%
7th Grade	75%	71%	−4%	15%	12%	−3%
8th Grade	61%	85%	+24%	21%	16%	−5%
9th Grade	68%	74%	+6%	11%	6%	−5%
10th Grade	74%	74%	0%	10%	12%	+2%
11th Grade	82%	83%	+1%	7%	6%	−1%
12th Grade	85%	85%	0%	7%	5%	−2%

Source: Oregon Reading First Center, Center on Teaching and Learning, Portland, OR.

YOUR TURN

Use one of the above formats to evaluate effectiveness of instructional supports in your school.

- Identify an area to evaluate (reading or math) and the evaluation period (fall to winter or winter to spring). Also identify the grade or grades to be evaluated.

- What percentage of Benchmark/proficient students at each grade remained at Benchmark? Were any lost?

- What percentage of Strategic students moved to Benchmark? What percentage stayed at Strategic or fell into Intensive?

- What percentage of Intensive moved out of Intensive to either Strategic or Benchmark/proficient? What percentage stayed at Intensive?

Are There Unanswered Questions?

The methods presented for evaluating system effectiveness allow schools to examine how well systems are working by comparing the percentage of students in each category from one testing period to the next, such as winter to spring. Of course, the overall goal is to increase the percentage of students at Benchmark (low risk) and decrease the percentage of students at Intensive (high risk). Despite the value and impact such comparisons provide, several important questions may remain unanswered:

- Where did students move when falling out of Benchmark or rising from Intensive?
- Which students and groups of students moved the most?
- How much movement is adequate?
- What is considered an acceptable rate level of growth?

WHAT IS ADEQUATE PROGRESS?

Adequate progress is a way to quantify the effectiveness of systems. While system effectiveness could be evaluated in various ways, this chapter focuses on two approaches: (1) risk reduction and (2) percentile score improvement.

In the first approach, adequate progress is measured as a function of how many students change risk categories, moving from a high level of risk to a lesser degree of risk. At the secondary school level, reducing risk (Intensive to Strategic or Strategic to Benchmark/proficient) has important implications for predicting success in everything from passing content area classes to predicting student performance on end-of-course exams, passing state achievement tests, performance on ACT, and so on.

Risk reduction is evaluated by comparing the change of students across risk categories from one benchmark period to the next (fall to winter or winter to spring). For a given school, the effectiveness of intensive interventions (the Intensive System) would be measured by comparing the percentage of students moving from Intensive to Strategic or Intensive to Benchmark. Likewise, the percentage of students moving from Strategic to Benchmark would be a measure of their Strategic system's effectiveness.

Using the above method, there are two ways to measure system effectiveness:

1. Intensive students moving to Strategic or Benchmark

2. Strategic students moving to Benchmark

Evaluating progress using this first method requires simply calculating the percentage of students who change risk categories from one benchmark period to the next. If a schools has forty Intensive ninth graders (in reading) in the fall and twenty of those students move out of that risk level to either Strategic or Benchmark by winter, 50 percent of the Intensive students would be considered to have made substantial progress. If ten of the original forty Intensive students move to a lower risk category (Strategic or Benchmark), 25 percent would have made substantial progress. This method requires evaluating the movement of intact groups of students— only students at the school for both benchmark assessments would be included in the calculation.

A second method for evaluating progress, Percentile Score Improvement, is to count the number of students who make a minimum of a ten-percentile-point gain from one testing period to the next. A ten-percentile-point gain would be considered significant growth—the number of students achieving such growth would be used as a measure of a system's effectiveness. For instance, if four of thirteen Strategic eighth-grade students scored ten or more percentile points higher on the winter benchmark assessment compared to fall, 31 percent of the Strategic eighth-grade students would have achieved substantial progress. Similarly, if out of nine Intensive sixth graders none made a minimum of ten-point-percentile gain from fall to winter, no students would have made substantial progress. Again, only students included in both benchmark assessments would be included in the calculation. Students who move into the school or move out would not be included.

Interpreting Adequate Progress

With a working definition of adequate progress, schools can easily calculate the percentage of students making adequate progress or expected growth. The next step is to identify a percentage of students a system can realistically expect to make such progress. In other words, what percentage of students should be expected to make substantial progress for a system to be considered effective?

The following criteria are intended to be used as a guide for evaluating systems. Experience working with secondary schools and evaluating secondary systems is used as the basis for the criteria provided.

- 60 percent or more students achieving substantial progress = Above expected growth
- 30 percent to 59 percent students achieving substantial progress = Expected growth
- Less than 30 percent of students achieving adequate progress = Below expected growth

According to the above criteria, if a school's Intensive math system results in 62 percent of its Intensive students making a minimum of a 10 percentile gain from one testing period to the next, that system is considered highly effective. If, on the other hand, only 21 percent of the Intensive math students made a minimum of a 10 percentile gain, the system would be considered in need of improvement. As discussed, the school's departmental team or RTI team would be responsible for problem solving ways to improve particular systems such as math.

The template below can be a useful tool for a building or district to use when evaluating systems' effectiveness. The percentages of students making adequate progress (using either method described earlier) are entered then color-coded according to the values described above. Systems with above expected growth are color-coded blue; systems with expected growth are color-coded green; Systems with below expected growth are color-coded red. Schools then use the color coding to help prioritize which systems to address. Systems coded green are considered Healthy. Systems coded yellow and especially red are in need of improvement. Systems can sometimes be addressed by making minor changes, whereas others require total overhauls.

Effective Systems: Identifying Concerns

School	System-level Progress	6th	7th	8th	9th	10th	11th	12th	Strategic	Intensive
Middle School A	Strategic	65%	41%	23%					43%	59%
	Intensive	72%	49%	56%						

1. Identify the percentage of students at each grade who made adequate progress.

2. Identify the percentage of students across all grades at each risk level who made adequate growth.

3. Color-code each according to growth:
   o 60 percent or more made adequate growth = Blue
   o 30 percent to 59 percent made adequate growth = Green
   o Less than 30 percent made adequate growth = Red

Discussion

The completed template summarizes a school's adequate progress from fall to winter. The numbers recorded reveal the percentage of students who achieved adequate growth (the students who gained 10 percentile points or more on benchmark tests from fall to winter). The color coding is used to identify and rate system effectiveness—systems color-coded blue are working very well; color-coded green are effective, and color-coded red are in need of immediate problem solving. Using the above example, the data and color coding reveal both Intensive and Strategic sixth-grade systems are working very well, whereas the Strategic eighth-grade system is in need of improvement. The seventh-grade Strategic and Intensive systems as well as the eighth-grade Intensive systems are effective.

The color coding can serve as a powerful visual and way to communicate data. For many teams, this process can provide a useful format to evaluate systems; answering the question, which systems are working and to what degree. This is a beginning point for problem solving and making improvement to secondary systems that, however well intended, may go unchecked and unimproved.

Is Progress Sustained Over Time?

An effective system requires a sustained, coordinated effort across grades. Care must be taken to ensure within-year growth is sustained from one year to the next. The following graph illustrates the increase in the percentage of students at Benchmark and the decrease in the percentage of students at Intensive from Grade 6 through Grade 11. Despite the variability in performance from one benchmark testing period to another, the trendline indicates an increase in the percentage of students at Benchmark and a decrease in the percentage of students at Intensive. The trend lines reflect system effectiveness overtime . . . more students at proficient and fewer students in the intensive range.

Next Steps

After completing a review of grade and schoolwide progress reports, the information obtained will guide department-, grade-, or building-level RTI teams to focus on systems not meeting expected progress levels. The review process should identify support structures color-coded red for problem-solving priorities. Support structures coded yellow and green receive less priority than those color coded red.

The average percentage of students making adequate progress in each category is a logical starting point for the RTI team review of schoolwide

Tracking Instructional Recommendation

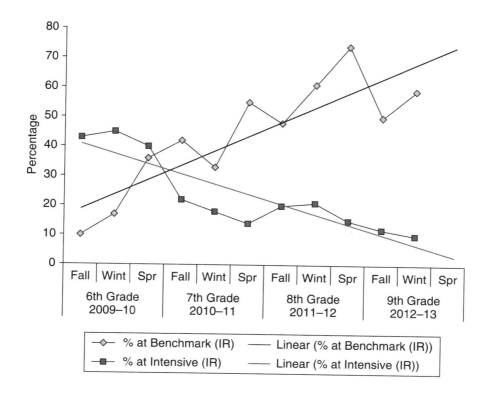

YOUR TURN

ADEQUATE PROGRESS: EVALUATING SYSTEMS/COLOR CODING—ACTIVITY 7

Complete for using your own school's data:

1. Use your school's reading or math scores to complete the Adequate Progress worksheet below.

2. What percentage of Intensive and Strategic students made adequate growth at each grade?

3. Using green, yellow, and red markers, color-code each grade and level of support according to the following scale:

   60 percent or more made adequate progress = Green

   (Continued)

(Continued)

> 30 percent to 59 percent made adequate progress = Yellow
>
> Less than 30 percent made adequate progress = Red

4. Color-code each grade's total percentage of students making adequate growth for each system.

5. Calculate the average percentage of students making adequate growth for both the Intensive and Strategic systems (all grades).

6. Color-code each system using the above criteria.

7. Identify which systems are effective and which ones require additional support. Do some grades or systems require more support than others?

8. Finally, what specific conversations might teachers have regarding the results?

School	System-level Progress	6th	7th	8th	9th	10th	11th	12th	Strategic	Intensive
Middle School A	Strategic									
	Intensive									

progress. Examples of system-wide concerns include Intensive students across multiple grade levels not achieving expected growth. Isolated concerns might include Strategic-level students in only one grade failing to achieve expected growth for a semester.

Provided are two system-level checklists that can be used by RTI teams to help identify possible variables to change and improve systems/support structures.

RTI Implementation Checklist

Use this checklist to identify if specific elements are in place. Each element would be considered fully established only if all the sub items under each element are in place. Have multiple RTI team members and teachers complete the checklist then compare answers. Is everyone is agreement? Can each items answered "yes" be verified?

RTI IMPLEMENTATION CHECKLIST—SECONDARY SCHOOLS

	Elements of a Schoolwide Approach	YES	NO	PARTIAL	Comments
1.	Arrange system to meet the needs of students, including those with reading and math skill deficits.				
	A. Are reading and math interventions available for students with skill deficits?				
	B. Strategic-level students receive targeted intervention to address specific areas of need.				
	C. Intensive students are placed in comprehensive interventions for one to two class periods per day, five days per week.				
	D. Is a sufficient number of staff allocated?				
	E. Has staff been assigned in a way such that necessary interventions can be delivered to the full range of students each day?				
2.	Use universal screening and functional assessment (e.g., phonics screening, etc.) to identify and place students according to instructional needs.				
	A. Screening assessments are administered to identify students with math and/or reading skill deficits.				
	B. Diagnostic assessments are used to identify specific instructional focus for Strategic level students.				
	C. Intensive-level students are administered placement tests.				
3.	Use differentiated instruction to meet the needs of instructional groups.				
	A. Are students grouped according to identified instructional focus area (homogenously by performance level/skill deficits)?				
	B. Are students grouped based on program recommendation?				
	C. Are group sizes appropriate to ensure student success in intervention?				
4.	Use research-based interventions and instructional practices.				
	A. All instructional reading/math programs and materials are research validated.				
	B. Instructional programs are aligned to student instructional needs.				
	C. Are intervention programs implemented with fidelity?				
	D. Are fidelity checks conducted regularly?				
5.	Conduct frequent progress monitoring to ensure adequate growth.				
	A. In-program assessment (i.e., end of unit tests, etc.) are administered as required?				
	B. Out-of-program assessments are administered (monthly for Strategic students and twice monthly for Intensive students).				
	C. Data are used for instructional decision making (i.e., to adjust instructional groups, evaluate effectiveness of instruction, etc.).				
	D. Data meetings have been established and occur regularly.				

	Elements of a Schoolwide Approach	YES	NO	PARTIAL	Comments
6.	Provide ongoing professional development to support system-wide structures of instruction.				
	A. Is training provided for teachers (i.e., staff receives adequate training prior to teaching programs)?				
	B. Are program specific consultants brought in to observe in classrooms and provide ongoing support and training?				
	C. Are in-service sessions developed around implementation issues identified by the building/district administrators?				
	D. Do building administrators conduct classroom walk-throughs during intervention?				
	E. Are new teachers provided the necessary program training?				
7.	Use data to evaluate effectiveness of schoolwide system.				
	A. Does the school have a method to evaluate effectiveness of instructional supports/systems (i.e., Benchmark, Strategic, and Intensive)?				
	B. Less effective systems are identified and addressed (improved).				
	C. A schoolwide team is established to evaluate the effectiveness of systems.				
8.	Use problem-solving teams to identify and address unhealthy systems.				
	A. Building-level teams identify systems in need of support and are skilled at identifying actions to improve systems.				
	B. Action plans are created to address improve systems.				
	C. Outcome goals and evaluation methods are identified to evaluate the effectiveness of action plans.				
9.	Develop intervention plans for students whose needs cannot be adequately addressed within the system (e.g., require intervention/instruction not available as part of the overall system).				
	A. Intervention plans are created using a formal problem-solving process.				
	B. Goals of student intervention plans are clearly specified and regularly monitored.				
	C. Students in need of intervention are first addressed at the system level before being referred to the building-level team.				
	D. Student-level teams exist for the purpose of improving student performance rather than for referral.				
10.	Use information relevant to a student's response to intervention (progress-monitoring data, review of intervention duration, intensity, and fidelity) as part of process for determining eligibility for special education.				
	A. Students considered for special education have received intervention within effective systems.				
	B. Students considered for special education have received research validated interventions aligned to their instructional needs and for an extended period of time.				
	C. Progress-monitoring information, history of interventions, and results are used in determining eligibility for special education.				

The ICEL/RIOT Checklist

The ICEL Checklist and Summary Forms are used to assist the RTI team to identify and summarize factors contributing to student outcomes. Instruction, Curriculum, and Environment (ICE) are system-level elements, whereas Learner relates to individual students. RIOT is an acronym for the various ways information can be obtained (Review, Interview, Observe, and Test).

The questions under each of the ICEL domains are intended to help teams identify factors related to effective systems. For individual students, questions guide teams in collecting information relevant for problem solving. For the ICE system, begin with items under the heading titled Review. Ask: Are there items that are either not in place or that are uncertain? To what degree they are in place, identify items that require additional information and then identify what method will be used for collecting additional information (Interview, Observe, Test). Use the ICEL Summary Form to organize information collected from identified questions. The ICEL Summary Form allows reporting of information obtained according to the domain (ICEL) and method of collection (RIOT).

Use the ICEL/RIOT Checklist to help evaluate systems and individual students.

- Use the ICEL/RIOT Checklist to help identify what system-level (ICE) elements you have questions about or for which you need more information.
- Use the ICEL/RIOT Summary to report and analyze information collected after completing the ICEL Checklist.

ICEL/RIOT Checklist

Assessment Procedures/Data Sources

	R (Review)	I (Interview)	O (Observe)	T (Test/Assess)
	SYSTEMS PROBLEM SOLVING: Determine effectiveness of each part of the system by asking: 1. Is it effective at each level of the schoolwide system? 2. Is it effective at the instructional group level? 3. Is it effective for individual students?			
Instruction **I**	☐ Differentiated instruction is utilized to address the skill level needs of students (that is, Benchmark, Strategic, Intensive) ☐ Have instructors received ample, high quality training needed to provide instruction? ☐ Is adequate time available to teach students according to instructional needs? ☐ Is additional time available for student in need? ☐ Are instructors incorporating features of strong instruction (e.g., modeling, scaffolding, explicit directions, multiple opportunities to respond, etc.)? ☐ Are behavioral expectations explicitly taught? ☐ Are the most critical features being prioritized and taught? ☐ What percentage of students is making adequate progress? ☐ Are a high percentage of students making adequate progress? ☐ Is an appropriate range of programs available for all students? ☐ Are the program/materials appropriate for the instructional group? ☐ Are programs and instructional materials research based? Basis for conclusion?	☐ Is additional instructional time provided as necessary? ☐ Does the instructor feel adequately trained and supported to meet the needs of students? ☐ Is instruction differentiated? ☐ Is instruction adequately explicit with opportunities for students to practice? ☐ Are other students (e.g., students in the same instructional group) making adequate progress? What percentage? ☐ Are students highly successful during instruction (90%+)? ☐ Are instructors adequately trained in delivery of programs/instructional materials? ☐ What are exceptions of strengths or limits of programs/materials? ☐ Does the programming available match the instructional needs of the learners?	☐ Is instruction differentiated (like students grouped together)? ☐ Is the instruction direct and explicit: includes modeling actively engaging all students? ☐ Are students provided with extensive opportunities to respond during instruction? ☐ Are students given ample opportunities to practice skills being taught? ☐ Is corrective feedback provided? ☐ Are reinforcing statements provided to encourage student effort and response? ☐ Are all students in the group responding and completing activities with a high level of performance? ☐ Are students appropriately grouped and placed in the program/materials? ☐ Do program/materials promote a high degree of student response? ☐ Are students successful in the program/materials? ☐ Is the program appropriate for the group and purpose for which it is intended (Benchmark, Strategic, Intensive)?	☐ All students in the instructional group are passing in-program or instructionally based assessments? ☐ Are students progressing through content at expected rate (for example, 1 lesson per day, etc.)? ☐ Are students mastering content? ☐ Is program/materials content generalized—students demonstrate ability to apply skills taught (for example, as measured by CBM, AIMSweb, social skills, etc.)?

146

		R (Review)	I (Interview)	O (Observe)	T (Test/Assess)
C	**Curriculum**	☐ Are all necessary programs/materials available? ☐ Are programs/instructional materials implemented with fidelity? ☐ Does the curriculum match the instructional priorities established for the learner? ☐ Does the design and delivery of the program/materials ensure the instructional group is highly successful? ☐ Are the programs/materials systematic and explicit?	☐ Are students appropriately grouped according to the program guidelines?	☐ Is the instructor skilled in delivery of content? ☐ Are students highly engaged in program/materials during delivery of instruction?	☐ Do program/materials need to be evaluated to determine effectiveness? ☐ Are program/materials designed for the purpose for which they are being used? ☐ Does alignment exist between what's being taught and the learning needs of students? ☐ Is curriculum aligned to state and local standards and benchmarks?
E	**Environment**	☐ Are positive, proactive behavioral supports in place? ☐ What is the average number of behavioral referrals for grade? Within each class? ☐ Are teachers and support staff trained in positive and effective behavior management practices? ☐ Does scheduling minimize interruptions during instructional periods? ☐ Are instructional materials available and well managed? ☐ Are routines and expectations directly taught and periodically reviewed? ☐ Are new staff members trained in the school's behavioral support philosophy/system? ☐ Are supports and interventions available for students with greater behavioral challenges?	☐ Do teacher(s) feel well-trained/supported in the school's disciplinary methodology? ☐ Are learning environments well organized and minimize distractions? ☐ Are behavioral expectations directly taught and periodically reviewed with students? ☐ Are routines well understood by students? ☐ Are students successful in their learning environments? ☐ Are students highly engaged in their learning? ☐ Are additional supports available for students with behavioral concerns?	☐ Do physical arrangements of rooms facilitate learning? ☐ Is there a 5 to 1 praise to consequence ratio? ☐ Are students successful in academic tasks? ☐ Are students highly engaged during lesson and academic tasks? ☐ Are students grouped homogenously? ☐ Are behavioral expectations taught and positively reinforced? ☐ Are lessons free of interruptions (for example, announcements, assemblies, etc.)	☐ Have you conducted a rate of students' response survey—evaluated extent of engagement during lesson instruction? ☐ Are students 90 percent accurate when responding during lessons? ☐ Do students understand behavioral expectations?
INDIVIDUAL PROBLEM SOLVING					
		☐ Are there any medical or developmental concerns reported in the student's cumulative folder? ☐ Has the student been present 95 percent or more of instructional days?	☐ What does student report as their strengths and weaknesses? ☐ What are the student's likes and dislikes?	☐ How does the student's behavior compare to his or her peers? ☐ Does the student have frequent opportunities to respond to tasks during teacher directed instruction? ☐ How is the student's time on-task?	☐ Has a hearing or vision problem been ruled out? If so, when was the last evaluation?

(Continued)

(Continued)

	R (Review)	I (Interview)	O (Observe)	T (Test/Assess)
L **Learner**	☐ Does the student have a history of school or class tardiness? ☐ Has the student received passing grades on their report card? ☐ When did the problem begin? ☐ How long has this been a problem? ☐ What have previous teachers reported about the problem? ☐ What is the standard performance of peers? ☐ Does the cumulative record indicate a pattern of behavior? ☐ Do the cumulative records reflect any interference with personal, interpersonal, and academic adjustment? ☐ What are the settings where the behavior of concern has occurred? ☐ Is there a pattern of performance that indicates skills deficits? ☐ What has previous progress monitoring revealed about student's learning patterns? ☐ What are the interventions have the student shown resistance to? ☐ What interventions have been attempted? What were the results?	☐ What are the student's views on the problem? ☐ How does the student think the problem could be corrected? ☐ What are the parents' biggest concerns for their child? ☐ What are the teacher's perceptions of the problem? ☐ How does the teacher rate the intensity of the problem? ☐ What is the parents' perception of the problem? ☐ How do the parents rate the intensity of the problem? ☐ Is there a pattern of behavior perceived by parents, teachers, and student? ☐ Is there a common setting to the behavior of concern? ☐ Are similar concerns reported by other teachers or staff members who interact with this student? ☐ Why is this particular student not progressing at a rate similar to other students? ☐ What would be required to make the instruction more effective for this student?	☐ Does the student talk without permission? ☐ Is the student physically aggressive (biting, hitting, spitting)? If yes, what is the frequency of the occurrences? In what context does the behavior occur? What are the antecedents and consequences of the behavior? ☐ Does the student engage in positive self-talk? ☐ Does the student engage in noise making (pencil tapping, humming)? ☐ What is the student's completion time relative to his or her peers? ☐ Does the student receive positive feedback? ☐ Is there a good match between the learner and the instructional methods? ☐ Does the student receive positive corrective practice in the areas of concern? ☐ Does the student receive individual attention from the teacher? ☐ What percentage of the time is the student compliant with classroom rules? ☐ Is the student successful during instruction? ☐ Is the student provided a correction procedure when in error? What is the student's response? ☐ Is the student motivated to perform? ☐ Does the student have positive peer/adult interactions?	☐ What is the student's instructional level? ☐ Has functional and diagnostic assessment pinpointed areas of need for instruction and been reassessed? ☐ Is the student missing prerequisite skills necessary for proficient performance in the targeted area? ☐ How does the student perform on individual skill assessments? ☐ What is the student's performance on classroom assessment? ☐ What are the student's specific skill strengths and weaknesses? ☐ What needs to be taught? ☐ What needs to be reinforced? ☐ What motivates this student?

ICEL/RIOT Summary Form

ICEL/RIOT Summary Form					
		Identify which items from the ICEL/RIOT checklist were relevant to the system(s) of concern.			
I Instruction	Systems/Groups	❑ ❑ ❑ ❑	❑ ❑ ❑ ❑	❑ ❑ ❑ ❑	❑ ❑ ❑ ❑
C Curriculum		❑ ❑ ❑ ❑	❑ ❑ ❑ ❑	❑ ❑ ❑ ❑	❑ ❑ ❑ ❑
E Environment		❑ ❑ ❑ ❑	❑ ❑ ❑ ❑	❑ ❑ ❑ ❑	❑ ❑ ❑ ❑
L Learner for individual problem solving	Individual Student	❑ ❑ ❑ ❑	❑ ❑ ❑ ❑	❑ ❑ ❑ ❑	❑ ❑ ❑ ❑

EVALUATE AND PROBLEM SOLVE INSTRUCTIONAL GROUPS

Once levels of supports are evaluated for effectiveness at the systems level, a more in-depth examination must be made at the instructional group level.

Students in need of additional support are placed in instructional/ intervention groups/classes based on results of screening measures, skill analysis, and intervention placement testing. Instruction is designed to meet the needs of the instructional group. Grade-level, departmental, or RTI teams review data to determine whether supports are adequately effective for the majority of students in each group.

To evaluate and problem solve instructional groups

- Begin by targeting groups within grades and systems that showed the least amount of growth (systems color-coded red).
- For each grade or system, use progress-monitoring measures (in-program or CBM measures) to evaluate the growth of each group. Identify instructional groups that do not have the majority (80%) of students progressing as anticipated.
- Identify possible reasons for the lack of progress by using the ICEL Checklist. Then use a problem-solving process to find solutions that will improve the performance of the group.

Evaluating the Progress of Instructional Groups

1. Evaluate the progress of each group according to preestablished aimline or anticipated rate of growth.

2. Determine whether supports are effective for most students within the group.

3. Gauge whether 80 percent of students are progressing at the anticipated rate.

4. Use data to examine reasons for lack of progress.

Identifying Concerns at the Group Level

1. Use benchmark and progress-monitoring data to identify which instructional groups are not making adequate progress.

2. Use the ICEL Checklist to identify possible reasons for the inadequate progress.

3. Use the ICEL Checklist and Alterable Variables Chart to identify possible changes that could be made to the instructional programming.

Initial Questions to Answer

1. Are we teaching and targeting the right skills and concepts?

2. Are we covering enough content to allow students to progress at the anticipated rate?

3. Are students learning what is being taught?

4. Are students retaining or generalizing what has been taught?

Question 1: Are We Teaching/Targeting the Right Skills/Concepts?

Determine the learning outcomes for each instructional group. Ensure Strategic students are having skill deficits directly addressed. For Intensive students, ensure that students are in a comprehensive, research-validated intervention and placed in groups according to individual and instructional level needs.

Question 2: Are We Covering Enough Content?

Pacing schedules ensure that consideration is given to how much content needs to be covered for students to achieve targeted end-of-semester or end-of-year outcomes. In other words, a student's response to intervention depends directly on how much content has been covered (see table below). If students are starting Corrective Reading B1, 65 lessons must be completed, which would equal a 3.5 grade-level outcome.

Program Level and Grade Equivalent Outcomes (Corrective Reading)

Students Working (Lesson Progress)	Grade Level Outcome
Corrective Reading Level A (65 lessons)	2nd Grade
Corrective Reading Level B1 (65 lessons)	3.5 Grade
Corrective Reading Level B2 (65 lessons)	4.8 Grade
Corrective Reading Level C (120 lessons)	7th Grade

Effective pacing ensures students are learning and generalizing content as it is being taught. To simply move through lessons in the pursuit of completing a series is not the goal and, indeed, is an exercise in futility. Strategic pacing, on the other hand, allows educators to plan the amount of instructional time according to the needs of the group. In addition to careful monitoring of student progress, pacing is critical to both students' response to intervention and closing the achievement gap.

Question 3: Are Students Learning What Has Been Taught?

Teachers incorporate informal and ongoing assessment of student learning to ensure understanding during instruction, including choral and individual responses, monitoring independent work, listening to students read, and so on. Formal assessments are also administered to ensure student understanding and mastery of content. Such assessments include end of unit tests, chapter tests, mastery checks, skill checkouts, and so on. In-program assessment is conducted for the purpose of informing instruction and answering whether students are learning what is being taught.

> Consider . . . Nothing has been taught until something has been learned.

Question 4: Are Students Generalizing What Has Been Taught?

Can students apply the skills to situations outside the setting in which they were taught—can they really *do* it?

To answer this question, educators should use out-of-program monitoring such as Curriculum-Based Measurement (CBM) or content sampling techniques. Such measures evaluate students' ability to apply the skills. Automaticity is considered a key component when evaluating a student's ability to apply a previously learned task. For instance, EasyCBM Passage Reading Fluency assesses how well a student has learned and integrated complex reading skills by measuring his or her ability to read connected text with automaticity.

A Tool for Tracking Student Progress

Kidgraph is a tool for monitoring group and individual student learning. It allows educator's to plan and track student learning regarding pacing, mastery, and generalizing. In short, Kidgraph allows educators to track the four questions listed above, both at the group and individual student levels.

Kidgraph is an electronic evaluation system that assesses learning by incorporating in-program and out-of-program assessments to ensure students not only learn program content but are also able to apply newly acquired skills to everyday learning (e.g., apply newly acquired advanced phonic skills to read a grade-level passage).

Features of Kidgraph

Monitors learning at the instructional group and individual student levels

- Individual student performance is tracked and displayed electronically but viewed in the context of and in comparison to the instructional group.

Creates pacing maps (amount of content to be taught)

- Allows teams or teachers to plan and track pacing of the instructional group.

Maximizes the potential of instructional programs

- Provides information of whether (a) enough content is being covered, (b) students are learning skills taught, (c) students are generalizing newly acquired skills, and (d) whether the intervention/instruction is generally effective for the group and each individual student within the group.

Provides an easy to read visual display of data as they are entered

- Provides immediate data feedback.

Is uniquely suited for RTI

- Kidgraph provides information relative to a student's intervention history, including a list of interventions applied and completed, comprehensive tracking of in-program performance, pacing (amount of content completed), performance on out-of-program monitoring (for example, DIBELS), days absent, behavior, and a performance comparison to the instructional group.

Is easy to use

- Data are easily entered within minutes by teachers or teacher assistants.

The following is an example of Kidgraph:

Monitoring Instructional Groups
Kidgraph Form 1

Group Instructor: Beck   Program: Corrective Reading B-1

Grade/Group: 6th – Gray   Date: 10/15/09

Expected Lesson#_113

Actual Lesson #_107

Student Name	Passed Mastery Tests?	On Aimline?		Behavior +/-	Days Absent	Comments:
Javaris	Y	Y		+	2	
Willy	Y	Y		+	0	
Jamal	N	Y		+	4	Failed last two mastery tests
Leticia	Y	Y		+	1	Passed retest
Jani	N	N		+	0	Passed retest
Duane	Y	Y		+	0	
Devon	Y	Y		+	0	
Marrisa	N	Y		+	2	Passed all previous mastery tests
Kimberly	Y	Y		-	0	
Anthony	Y	Y		+	0	
Toni	Y	Y		+	1	
Alee	Y	Y		+	0	
Percentage of students Passing or on Aimline?	83	92				

To purchase Kidgraph or to find out more, go to Partnersforlearning.org or contact Partners for Learning, Inc. (208) 322–5007.

When Problem Solving, Consider the Following

- Structural Problems
    - Instructional time
    - Grouping of students
    - Staffing
    - Lesson pacing

- Implementation Problems
    - Fidelity to the program
    - Content pacing: mastery

- Generalization problems
    - Opportunities to respond

- System Problems
    - Ineffective programs
    - One-size-fits-all
    - Philosophical differences
    - Competing programs or interventions
    - Uncoordinated or inconsistent instruction
    - General features of instruction (modeling, explicit language, etc.)

ESTABLISHING A PACING SCHEDULE

EXAMPLE: PACING SCHEDULE

Create a pacing schedule for Mrs. Andrew's eighth-grade Intensive students. They must complete Corrective Reading B2, lesson 65, by the end of May. It is November, and the group just completed Lesson 17. Identify a pacing schedule that will predict when all sixty-five lessons will be completed.

HOW MANY WEEKS? 24

3 November

2 December

4 January

4 February

3 March

4 April

4 May

HOW MANY LESSONS? 48

65 − 17 = 48

(Continued)

(Continued)

WHAT IS THE AVERAGE NUMBER OF LESSONS PER WEEK? 5

48 / 5 = 9.6 week

COMPLETED EXAMPLE: IDENTIFIED TARGET LESSONS FOR NOVEMBER, DECEMBER, JANUARY, AND FEBRUARY.

November: through Lesson 32

December: through Lesson 47

January: through Lesson 65

As you can see from the example pacing schedule above, calculations were made to ensure that students reach Lesson 65 by the end of May. To ensure pacing schedules are realistic, make sure students are correctly placed into the correct level of intervention, enough time per day is devoted to cover the number of lessons necessary to keep up with daily, weekly, and monthly pacing schedules. For maximum progress, consider scheduling two periods per day for the intervention. There is benefit to splitting the periods so they are not consecutive.

Example Group-Level Problem-Solving Forms and Action Plans

Schoolwide Instructional Effectiveness		
Description of Instructional Programming		
Academic Subject:	**Grade Level:**	**Date:**
School Practices	*Students at and Somewhat Below Grade Level*	*Students Significantly Below Grade Level*
1. Program materials used during the main instructional time	Materials used during whole-class instruction	Materials used during whole-class instruction
	Materials used during small-group instruction	Materials used during small-group instruction

School Practices	Students at and Somewhat Below Grade Level	Students Significantly Below Grade Level
2. Time when main instructional period begins and ends	Begins at _____ Ends at _____ Total Minutes _____	Begins at _____ Ends at _____ Total Minutes _____
3. Minutes during the main instructional time that each student received teacher directed instruction in whole class instruction in small group instruction	_____ minutes of teacher-directed whole-class instruction during core time _____ minutes of teacher-directed small-group instruction provided to each student somewhat below grade level during core time _____ days a week.	_____ minutes of teacher-directed whole-class instruction during core time _____ minutes of teacher-directed small-group instruction provided to each student significantly below grade level during core time _____ days a week.
4. Extra minutes of teacher-directed instruction provided for students below grade level in addition to time during main period	_____ minutes of extra instruction provided to students somewhat below grade level (Strategic) _____ days a week.	_____ minutes of extra instruction provided to students significantly below grade level (Intensive) _____ days a week.
5. Programs and materials used during the extra teacher-directed small group time		
6. How often are progress-monitoring assessments administered in addition to Benchmark assessments?	Assessment How often administered assessment	Assessment How often administered assessment
7. Other assessments administered. How often? Include assessments from programs.	Assessment How often administered assessment	Assessment How often administered assessment

Source: Adapted from Jerry Silbert with permission.

Team Meeting Record Sheet (sample)

Grade Level 7th	Grade Date 1/7/13	Participants 7th Grade Team _____

Purpose of Meeting

To examine the progress of all high strategic seventh graders

Identify and Define the Concern

Only 35 percent of students in the seventh grade were able to reach the progress-monitoring targets for wcpm on fluency assessment passages. Students are still struggling to read with fluency.

Analyze the Concern (what needs to be taught)

Fluency building opportunities are not routinely included as part of intervention block.

Generate Actions/Solutions

1. Teachers will examine the types of errors made by their students.

2. Teachers will arrange schedules so that all students needing extra support will complete 6-Minute Solution fluency building exercises.

3. More frequent fluency assessments will be provided to students not on fluency aimlines.

4. Results will be analyzed in the next PLC meeting.

Specific Decisions/Solutions

Teachers will review each student's assessment of oral-reading fluency and make a chart indicating areas of need. Teachers will use the more frequent fluency-assessment passages and chart the progress.		
The instructor will have students complete 6-Minute Solution at the end of each intervention period.		
Continue small-group instruction. Continue weekly fluency assessments.		

Evaluation Method: Fluency assessments—weekly	**Next Meeting: 2/7/13**

Progress-Monitoring Groups of Students

YOUR TURN

EFFECTIVE PROBLEM SOLVING—ACTIVITY 8

1. Identify a system or instructional group within your building requiring support.

2. Complete the ICEL Checklist. Identify questions to be answered and information to be collected.

3. Collect the information and summarize the results on the Post-ICEL Assessment.

4. Identify elements that need to be addressed to strengthen that portion of the system. Complete the Team Meeting Record Sheet on the next page to help problem solve a solution and create an actionable plan to address the areas of identified concern.

PROBLEM SOLVING FOR INDIVIDUAL STUDENTS

A systems approach to RTI is structured to address students according to their instructional needs (Benchmark, Strategic, Intensive). At each level, students are placed in flexible, homogeneous groups according to skill level. Within each instructional grouping, progress monitoring is used to evaluate the effectiveness of the instructional programming. If the majority of students in the group are *not* making expected progress, such as in Group A below, system or group problem solving is initiated. Individual student problem solving is initiated when, as illustrated in Group B, the majority of the instructional group is making adequate progress, but one or two students are not.

Before problem solving individual students, teams should consider whether the student could be supported by simply modifying existing supports—such as adding additional practice, preteaching, and reteaching— or placed within another existing instructional group or support. Individual student problem solving, including development of an Intervention Plan (I-Plan) is used in circumstances where reasons for the student's difficulty need to be more clearly examined and, when intervention is not readily available within the existing structure of supports.

Group A

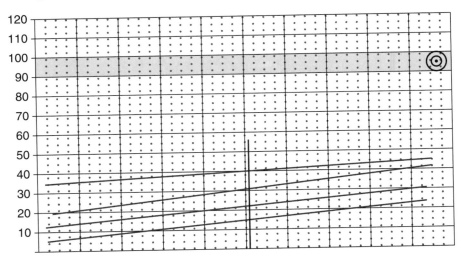

Group B

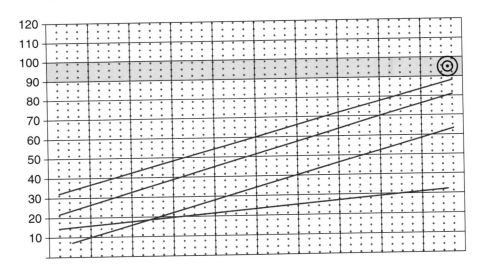

Systems Problem Solving vs. Individual Problem Solving

RTI Framework

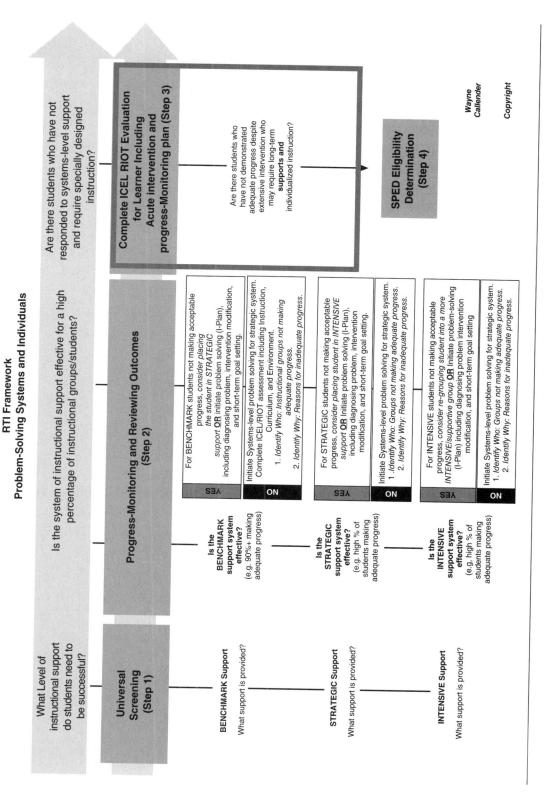

YOUR TURN

EFFECTIVE PROBLEM SOLVING—ACTIVITY 9

1. With a partner, review the Individual Students section of The RTI Team: Purpose and Process (See below in the Toolbox.).

2. Discuss each item and summarize the process for solving problems of individual students.

3. List questions you have about the process.

THE RTI TEAM: PURPOSE AND PROCESS

TEAM PURPOSE

1. Team consists of principal, departmental representatives, Title I, school psychologists, special education, and other specialists as needed.

2. Team meets at least once per month (45 mins.–2 hrs.)

3. Team reviews schoolwide data to evaluate health of system 3 times per year (fall, winter, spring).

4. Team shares results with departmental teams.

5. Team reviews progress of systems, by grade and department, to ensure systems improve and/or remain healthy.

6. Team engages in problem-solving systems, instructional groups, and individual students depending on the concern.

HEALTHY SYSTEMS

1. Review benchmark data in reading, writing, math and behavior. What percentage of students are Benchmark, Strategic, or Intensive?

2. Evaluate progress fall to winter and winter to spring for all grade levels. Identify systems requiring additional support (i.e., those with inadequate progress.

3. Evaluate progress of instructional groups. Target those with insufficient growth.

4. Collect information regarding system elements requiring further development by completing the ICEL/RIOT pre- and postassessment.

5. Problem-solve system solutions and create an action plan to increase support to identify concerns.

6. Establish benchmarks and timelines (i.e., monthly, quarterly) for evaluating success of improvement plan.

7. Periodically review progress toward benchmarks by evaluating progress of instruction groups monthly and modify the systems intervention plan as necessary.

INDIVIDUAL STUDENTS

1. Complete the Request for Problem Solving form, below.

2. Identify what systems supports were already provided and the results of interventions completed. Were there other students who failed to adequately progress? Was the system considered effective for the majority of students?

3. As a problem-solving team, identify what additional information must be obtained to understand the students presenting problem.

4. Complete the LEARNER portion of the ICEL/RIOT. Summarize the results on the POST-ICEL assessment.

Steps for Problem Solving at the Individual Student Level

There are four steps to problem solving at the individual student level:

1. Begin with a Request for Problem Solving Form.

2. Complete the ICEL/RIOT Learner section.

3. Review the effectiveness of the system.

4. As a team, write an Intervention Plan (I-Plan) that identifies the
   - problem,
   - goal for improvement,
   - research-based intervention,
   - implementation plan A and B,
   - progress-monitoring plan and decision rules,
   - follow-up date, and
   - case manager.

Step 1: Begin with the Request for Problem Solving form.

Request for problem solving is initiated when student progress is inadequate or when it is perceived that a student is in need of more support than is available in the existing system. The Request for Problem Solving form identifies the concern and what has already been tried, and it asks whether the parents have been contacted and are aware of the concern.

Request for Problem Solving—Student

(This form is to be completed by referring teacher prior to the team meeting)

Date of Referral: _____

School: _____   District: _____

Name _____   Date of Birth _____   Grade _____

Father/Guardian _____

Mother/Guardian _____

General Ed Teacher _____   Building Principal _____

1. What is the problem? (Be specific)

2. Describe what you would like the student to be able to do in class/school.

3. Describe what the student is currently doing. (Be specific.)

4. Describe what has been done to address the problem. List all interventions attempted as well as any adjustments made to interventions:

5. Would you like an observation to be completed before the intervention Team meeting? _____

   If yes, what is the best time/class period? _____

6. Indicate what you believe are the student's strengths, affinities, interests, and/or positive attributes.

7. Have the student's parents been contacted? _____   Are they aware of the concerns? _____

   Date of contact: _____

   What was their reply or response to concerns? _____

8. Is there additional information relevant to this student's concerns the team should be aware of?

Referring Source: _____   Date: _____

Step 2: Review the effectiveness of the system and previous interventions.

- Review adequate progress of the student's instructional group— did most other students make acceptable levels of growth?
- Were the supports required for this student available within the system?
- What additional supports (for example, double dose, changes to instruction, and so on) were provided in effort to bolster the student's progress?
- Are there system supports not currently available that could address this student's needs?
- Are there other students in the group who did not demonstrate adequate improvement? If so, would it be more efficient to problem solve as a group?

ICEL/RIOT

	INDIVIDUAL PROBLEM SOLVING			
L **Learner**	❑ Are there any medical or developmental concerns reported in the student's cumulative folder? ❑ Has the student been present 95 percent or more of instructional days? ❑ Does the student have a history of school or class tardiness? ❑ Has the student received passing grades on his or her report card? ❑ When did the problem begin? ❑ How long has this been a problem? ❑ What have previous teachers reported about the problem? ❑ What is the standard performance of peers? ❑ Does the cumulative record indicate a pattern of behavior? ❑ Do the cumulative records reflect any interference with personal, interpersonal, and academic adjustment? ❑ What are the settings where the behavior of concern has occurred? ❑ Is there a pattern of performance that indicates skills deficits? ❑ What has previous progress monitoring revealed about the student's learning patterns? ❑ What are the interventions that have the student has shown resistance to? ❑ What interventions have been attempted? What were the results?	❑ What does student report as his or her strengths and weaknesses? ❑ What are the student's likes and dislikes? ❑ What are the student's views on the problem? ❑ How does the student think the problem could be corrected? ❑ What are the parent's biggest concerns for their child? ❑ What are the teacher's perceptions of the problem? ❑ How does the teacher rate the intensity of the problem? ❑ What is the parents' perception of the problem? ❑ How do the parents rate the intensity of the problem? ❑ Is there a pattern of behavior perceived by parents, teachers, and student? ❑ Is there a common setting to the behavior of concern? ❑ Are similar concerns reported by other teachers or staff members who interact with this student? ❑ Why is this particular student not progressing at a rate similar to other students? ❑ What would be required to make the instruction more effective for this student?	❑ How does the student's behavior compare to his or her peers'? ❑ Does the student have frequent opportunities to respond to tasks during teacher-directed instruction? ❑ How is the student's time on-task? ❑ Does the student talk without permission? ❑ Is the student physically aggressive (biting, hitting, spitting)? If yes, what is the frequency of the occurrences? In what context does the behavior occur? What are the antecedents and consequences of the behavior? ❑ Does the student engage in positive self-talk? ❑ Does the student engage in noise making (pencil tapping, humming)? ❑ What is the student's completion time relative to his or her peers? ❑ Does the student receive positive feedback? ❑ Is there a good match between the learner and the instructional methods? ❑ Does the student receive positive corrective practice in the areas of concern? ❑ Does the student receive individual attention from the teacher? ❑ What percentage of time is the student compliant with classroom rules? ❑ Is the student successful during instruction? ❑ Is the student provided a correction procedure when in error? What is the student's response? ❑ Is the student motivated to perform? ❑ Does the student have positive peer/adult interactions?	❑ Has a hearing or vision problem been ruled out? If so, when was the last evaluation? ❑ What is the student's instructional level? ❑ Has functional and diagnostic assessment pinpointed areas of need for instruction and been reassessed? ❑ Is the student missing prerequisite skills necessary for proficient performance in the targeted area? ❑ How does the student perform on individual skill assessments? ❑ What is the student's performance on classroom assessment? ❑ What are the student's specific skill strengths and weaknesses? ❑ What needs to be taught? ❑ What needs to be reinforced? ❑ What motivates this student?

Step 3: Complete the Learner section from
the ICEL/RIOT and complete the Postassessment.

The ICEL Checklist will help you identify the additional information needed to understand the problem. The Postassessment will be used to summarize information obtained about the student during problem solving.

Step 4: Write an Intervention Plan.

- Identify the specific problem to be addressed.
- Establish a goal that reflects an ambitious degree of improvement.
- Identify how the problem will be measured.
- Specify the intervention to be implemented.
- Establish an implementation plan and timeline.
- Create a plan for monitoring progress along with decision rules to gauge intervention effectiveness.
- Establish a follow-up date.
- Identify the case manager to oversee implementation and evaluate progress monitoring.

An example intervention plan is on the next page. Detailed guidelines for developing an intervention plan begin below.

Example: RTI Intervention Plan

Student's Name _____ DOB _____ Age _____ Grade _____

Teacher _____ Date of Referral _____

Participants & Roles _____

I.   Identify the Concern

A. What is the specific concern? _____

_____

B. What system-level interventions have been tried? Results? _____

_____

C. Are there additional systems level supports that could be initiated? _____

_____

II.   Define the Problem

A. Measurement Strategy (circle one)

Duration   Event   Latency

1. What will be measured? _____

2. Measurement method? _____

B. Present level of performance:

1. Student's present level of performance _____

2. Benchmark/expectation _____

C. Problem Analysis

1. Review effectiveness of the system: is it working for most students and those with similar concerns/performances? _____

2. Complete ICEL/RIOT Learner assessments to identify skill deficits, answering these questions: _____

   a. It is a skill or performance problem? _____

   b. Results of Problem Analysis? _____

   c. What needs to be taught? _____

   d. Additional information? _____

III. Goal

A. Identify the desired outcome. _____

B. Identify the anticipated overall time frame to meet the desired outcome. _____

C. Identify an ambitious, but realistic rate of growth/progress. _____
_____

D. Write a nine-week goal. Include time frame materials, setting, student's name, behavior, and criterion. _____

PROBLEM SOLVING FOR
INDIVIDUAL STUDENTS: ESSENTIAL STEPS

KEYS TO SUCCESS

- Sense of urgency
- Specific goals and timeline
- Research-Validated Interventions
- Focus on alterable Variables
- A "Whatever it takes!" attitude

Step 1: Identify the Problem

Consider . . .

What is a Problem?

A problem is the difference between what is expected and the student's actual performance.

Example:

Expectation	Expect Gary to read 140 WPM with 0 errors.
Performance	Currently Gary reads 33 WPM with 5 errors.

Example:

Expectation	It is expected that Jentry raise her hand before asking a question 100 percent of the time.
Performance	Jentry raises her hand only 10 percent of the time.

A. Review information summarized on the ICEL/RIOT

Answer:

1. Are there system level concerns that should be addressed?

2. Were the student's original concerns validated?

3. From the information obtained, prioritize what will be addressed?

I-Plan

Post-Assessment: ICEL/RIOT

ICEL Assessment Summary

Mary Ann	Assessment Procedures/Data Sources			
	R (Review)	I (Interview)	O (Observe)	T (Test/Assess)
Systems/Groups				
I Instruction	• Students instructed on expected behavior (rules posted) • Data indicate most students are performing well • Social skills instruction not provided	• Struggling students receive extra assistance • Differentiated instruction utilized in math and reading • Instructions/expectations made clear to students	• Learning objective are clear • Lessons well-paced, organized	• Principles of effective instruction reviewed; 90 percent utilized
C Curriculum	No social skills curriculum Academic curriculum aligned to standards Curriculum outcomes generally met	• Teacher is satisfied with core curriculum • Teacher reports a separate social skills curriculum is not necessary	• Content of curriculum appears interesting to most students	
E Environment	• Environment well structured Discipline referrals 20 percent higher than school median	• Teacher reports environment is successful for most students • Teachers report Mary Ann sets a bad example for class—difficult to maintain structure when she does not comply with requests	• Moderate pressure for success is applied • Peer pressure used frequently • Peers observed to be compliant • Praise to consequence ratio 1 to 3	• ICEL Checklist indicates generally positive environmental attributes

I-Plan
Post-Assessment: ICEL/RIOT

Mary Ann	Assessment Procedures/Data Sources		ICEL Assessment Summary	
	R (Review)	I (Interview)	O (Observe)	T (Test/Assess)
Individual Student L Learner for individual problem solving	• Student's history reveals no behavioral concerns. • Academic skills are grade appropriate • Previous teachers report Mary Ann had few friends • Retained in first grade	• Teacher indicates rules are posted and reviewed • Student interview: does not like school/teachers • Parents report no problems at home • Problems reported in lunchroom and other less structured environments • Fewer concerns noted in other classrooms	• May Ann's compliance to teacher requests: In class, 32%; in all other classes, 68% • Mary Ann appears to be reinforced by attention from peers • Does not conform when consequences applied	• Student was able to explain expectations • CBM math and reading average • Student completed reinforcement inventory; likes reading, free time, basketball, and helping teachers

YOUR TURN

EFFECTIVE PROBLEM SOLVING: INDIVIDUALS—ACTIVITY 10

1. Mary Ann is a sixth-grade student. The school problem-solving team is meeting to complete an intervention plan. Prior to writing an intervention plan, information was collected using the ICEL/RIOT to help better understand the problem. Review the following information summarized on the Postassessment for Mary Ann.

2. From the information obtained, identify what information would be useful for a problem-solving team.

3. Are there system level concerns that should be addressed?

4. From the information summarized in the Learner domain above, what is the primary reason for Mary's lack of compliance behavior to teacher requests?

B. List and prioritize problems to be addressed

- Generate a list of problems specific to the individual.
- Prioritize the list based on guidelines for selection of target behaviors.
- Select the problem(s) of greatest importance as the target(s) for further assessment.

Prioritizing guidelines

- Target behaviors should be selected that maximize the individual's re-enforcers.
- Behaviors should be selected based on the skills the individual needs to develop.
- Consider what skills are needed in the next environment.
- Good target behaviors are enabling and important to others.

C. Behavioral Definition

A Behavioral Definition allows a problem to be defined in observable terms. It is descriptive enough that two observers could independently observe the same behavioral episodes and obtain similar observation data.

The Behavioral Definition Format is a useful tool for creating a common and consistent definition of a behavior. It identifies the name of the behavior and uses an action verb for describing how the behavior is to be operationalized. Below is an example of a Behavioral Definition Format:

Name of the behavior: _____

Means that . . .

Name of learner: _____

Action verbs describing what the learner is doing:

_____

_____

Examples include:

Describe what is to be counted: _____

YOUR TURN

GARY

- **Situation:** Gary is a seventh-grade student who is consistently off task. He is falling behind peers as a result of not paying attention and inconsistently completing his work.

- **Concern/behavior:** Excessively off task, leading to poor academic performance.

BEHAVIORAL DEFINITION FORMAT

Name of behavior: _off-task behavior_

Means that . . .

Name of learner: _Gary_

Action verbs describing what the learner is doing: _does not complete assignments on time_

(Continued)

(Continued)

Examples include:

Describe what is to be counted: *assignments turned in on time with 80 percent accuracy*

Non Examples include:

Describe what will not be counted: assignments not turned in on time, assignments completed with less than 80 percent accuracy, etc.

YOUR TURN

DAN, 9TH GRADE

- **Situation:** Dan is a ninth-grade student struggling in reading. His reading rate is slow because he struggles to sound out words.
- **Concern/behavior:** Reading fluency is 65 WPM compared to the expected rate of 135 WPM.

BEHAVIORAL DEFINITION FORMAT

Name of behavior: *difficulty reading*

Means that . . .

Name of learner: *Dan*

Action verbs describing what the learner is doing: reads 65 WPM compared to the expected rate of 135 wpm

Examples include:

Describe what is to be counted: words read correctly per minute _____

Describe what will not be counted: Comprehension, words read incorrectly, high frequency words, etc.

Use action verbs that are directly observable

Examples are as follows:

cover with a card	draw	say	mark
press lever	underline	point to	name
repeat orally	walk	tell what	shade
put on	circle	fill in	number
read orally	remove	label	state
place	cross out		

Do not use action verbs that are not directly observable

Examples are as follows:

distinguish	be curious	wonder	conclude
apply	analyze	develop	feel
deduce	concentrate	determine	learn
generate	think	know	think critically
discriminate	understand	recognize	appreciate
create	be aware of	become competent	test
discover	infer	realize fully	solve
like			

Avoid action verbs that are ambiguous

Examples are as follows:

identify in writing	check	summarize	match
take away	complete	arrange	finish
identify	play	locate	connect
give	reject	round off	choose
utilize	inquire	acknowledge	total
use	find	measure	construct
see	demonstrate	read	perform

YOUR TURN

EFFECTIVE PROBLEM SOLVING: INDIVIDUALS–ACTIVITY 11

1. Complete "Identify the Problem" for Mary Ann using the Behavioral Definition form and I-Plan.

2. Be sure to identify the problem in behavioral (observable) terms.

BEHAVIORAL DEFINITION FORMAT

Name of behavior: _____

Means that . . .

Name of learner: Mary Ann

Action verbs describing what the learner is doing:

Examples include:

Describe what is to be counted:

Non Examples include:

Describe what will not be counted:

Step 2: Define the Problem

Defining the problem requires completing three substeps:

- Select a measurement strategy.
- Identify the present level of performance.
- Analyze the problem.

Through identifying the above information, problem-solving teams are able to quantify and analyze a problem to better understand the underlying reasons for the problem. The goal is to understand the problem and match necessary interventions to improve student performance.

A. Select a measurement strategy.

A measurement strategy is a procedure used to collect individual performance data. The three recording strategies are as follows:

1. **Event:** Use event recording when the number of times something occurs is of interest. This requires the skill being measured to have a clear beginning and end. Example: count number of words read correctly, percentage of assignments completed, and so on.

2. **Duration:** Use duration recording when the concern is the length of time something occurs. Example: amount of time on task, length of time to complete an assignment, and so on.

3. **Latency:** Use latency recording when the concern is how long the student takes to begin behavior after a prompt. Example: time it takes a student to comply with a teacher request—time between request and compliance.

B. Identify the present level of performance.

The present level of performance (PLOP) describes an individual's baseline level of performance in a target behavior at a specific point in time. Subsequent performance will be compared to this baseline. The PLOP is required to set realistic, ambitious goals.

The data you use should be

Stable	Representative
Three to five measures that	The teacher says results
▶ are collected in appropriate settings, and	▶ are typical, and
▶ are collected within a relatively short time period.	▶ accurately describe the behavior as it naturally occurs.

Summarize the data

Use a median score. A median score is the middle—half of the scores are below that number and half are above it.

16, 22, 23	median = 22
114, 136, 140	median = 136
100, 107, 107	median = 107
32, 32, 32	median = 32
20, 24, 30, 31	median = 27

65, 72, 80   median = _____

48, 61, 62   median = _____

91, 92, 94, 95   median = _____

OUR TURN

DAN

1. **Measurement Strategy** = Event–Count number of words ready correctly.

2. **Present Level of Performance:** Mrs. Henry will use three grade-level reading probes to assess Dan's oral reading fluency. One probe will be given on three consecutive days.

RESULTS:

Day 1: 65 cwpm

Day 2: 34 cwpm

Day 3: 58 cwpm

Median = _____ cwpm

Analyze the Problem

What is problem analysis?

Problem analysis is the process used to examine probable explanations for the discrepancy between what the individual is expected to do and what the individual is doing.

Identified problems are often symptoms of a specific skill or performance deficit. Problem analysis is a method of breaking a problem down to examine and identify the nature or reason for the problem. When done well, it will help pinpoint the intervention to be applied. For example, poor reading is the presenting problem, but lack of decoding may be the actual reason for a student's poor reading skills. The intervention, then, is teaching missing decoding skills. In this way, problem analysis informs the intervention. Take, for example, off-task behavior. Problem analysis could be used to reveal a student's off-task behavior is actually a deficit in the ability to self-monitor during academic tasks.

SKILL OR PERFORMANCE?

IMPORTANT: The nature of a problem is domain-independent.

- Academic problems can be skill or performance related.
- Social-emotional problems can be skill or performance related.

Be sure to consider both possibilities for all problems.
When in doubt, treat problems as skill deficits.

Problems can be a skill or performance related, or both. A skill deficit means the student does not have the skill or is incapable of doing something, such as a student does not know his or her math facts. Skill deficits imply an instructional solution. A performance deficit, on the other hand, suggests a student is capable of doing something (has the skills) but does not perform or inconsistently performs. Example: a student is capable of writing a good book report, but does not do it because he or she is unmotivated to do so.

JEREMY HAS A READING PROBLEM.

Jeremy's median score on retelling details is 13. His peers' median score is 27 details.
Skill

- Needs additional instruction, practice, and feedback
- Needs to be taught comprehension strategies

Performance

- Can retell details
- Doesn't care whether he retells details
- Topic uninteresting to him
- Doesn't attend to errors

JILL HAS MANY PROBLEMATIC BUS BEHAVIORS.

Skill

- Has poor social skills
- Does not understand the rules

(Continued)

(Continued)

Performance

- Has the skills to follow the rules, but doesn't want to follow them
- Disobeying the rules is more reinforcing than following them.

How much diagnostic assessment should you do and when?

The primary purpose for diagnostic assessment is to identify what skills do and do not need to be taught. As mentioned in Chapter 3, Intensive students are often administered a placement test to identify entry into a comprehensive intervention. For such students, the placement test is often the only diagnostic assessment necessary. It identifies where the student's skills leave off and recommended placement in the intervention. The intervention then moves the student systematically from that point forward.

Conversely, Strategic students may have specific and isolated skill deficits that can be identified and targeted. Example: a teacher may use an assessment of comprehension to identify if a student's poor reading performance, as measured on the universal screener, is the result of literal or inferring difficulties. The comprehension assessment is the only diagnostic assessment used. It not only answers the questions about likely reasons for the student's poor reading, but it also identifies the precise skills to be targeted through instruction.

Examine probable explanations for the discrepancy and possible solutions

Apply this Problem Analysis format:

Problem analysis shows that if _____ is the problem (behavior), then_____will/should_____ (intervention) (effect/outcome/results of "problem").

OUR TURN

JULIA

Concern: Julia does not turn in assignments and is failing history.

Data-based Analysis: A review of Julia's academic skills and student interview revealed she is not motivated to turn in assignments.

Problem analysis shows that if motivation is the problem, then reinforcement of work completion will/should increase assignment completion.

YOUR TURN

ADAM

Concern: Off-task behavior.

Data-based Analysis: Diagnostic assessment revealed that Adam has difficulty self-monitoring.

Apply this format:

Problem analysis shows that if self-monitoring is the problem (behavior), then _____ will/should _____ (intervention) (effect/outcome/results of "problem").

YOUR TURN

EFFECTIVE PROBLEM SOLVING: INDIVIDUALS—ACTIVITY 12

Using information from the completed ICEL/RIOT Form, complete problem analysis for Mary Ann. Pay particular attention to the items in bold in the Learner category.

I-Plan

Post Assessment: ICEL/RIOT

Mary Ann—Assessment Procedures/Data Sources—ICEL Assessment Summary

Fill in the high priority, structural elements		R (Review)	I (Interview)	O (Observe)	T (test/assess)
I Instruction	Systems/Groups	Students instructed on expected behavior (rules posted) Data indicate most students are performing well Social skills instruction not provided	Struggling students receive extra assistance Differentiated instruction utilized in math and reading Instructions/ expectations made clear to students	Learning objective are clear Lessons well-paced, organized	Principles of effective instruction reviewed; 90 percent utilized
C Curriculum		No social skills curriculum Academic curriculum aligned to standards Curriculum outcomes generally met	Teacher is satisfied with core curriculum Teacher reports a separate social skills curriculum is not necessary	Content of curriculum appears interesting to most students	
E Environment		Environment well structured	Teacher reports environment is successful for most students	Moderate pressure for success is applied	ICEL Checklist indicates generally positive environmental attributes

Fill in the high priority, structural elements		R (Review)	I (Interview)	O (Observe)	T (test/assess)
		Discipline referrals 20 percent higher than school median	Teachers report Mary Ann sets a bad example for class—difficult to maintain structure when she does not comply with requests	Peer pressure used frequently Peers observed to be compliant Praise to consequence ratio 1 to 3	
L Learner for individual problem solving	Individual Student	Student's history reveals no behavioral concerns. Academic skills are grade appropriate Previous teachers report Mary Ann had few friends Retained in first grade	Teacher indicates rules are posted and reviewed Student interview: does not like school/teachers Parents report no problems at home Problems reported in lunchroom and other less structured environments Fewer concerns noted in other classrooms	Mary Ann's compliance to teacher requests: In class, 32%; in all other classes, 68% Mary Ann appears to be reinforced by attention from peers Does not conform when consequences applied	Student was able to explain expectations CBM math and reading average Student completed reinforcement inventory; likes reading, free time, basketball, and helping teachers

MARY ANN

Concern: _____

Data-Based Analysis: _____

Problem analysis shows that if _____ is the problem, then _____ will/should _____.

Step 3 Establish a Goal

The goal is the intended outcome of the intervention: the direction and extent to which the target behavior is to be changed within a time frame. The goal takes into account a student's PLOP and defines the method for monitoring progress.

What are benefits of goal writing?

Goal writing

- helps focus attention on whether the individual is making enough improvement,
- guides decision making about intervention effectiveness, and
- directs attention to the relative effectiveness of an intervention or instructional program.

What are the general characteristics of sound goals?

Specific

Measurable

Ambitious

Realistic

Take into account the expected performance

Set ambitious goals

Here's how to set an ambitious goal for increasing reading fluency.

- Identify starting words correct per minute (for example, 30 wcpm).
- Identify end-of-year grade-level target (for example, 90 wcpm).

- Subtract current wcpm from target and determine an amount of weekly growth required to meet the goal. Determine whether this is a realistic target (see Hasbrouk and Tindal [2005] growth chart).
- Set ambitious but realistic expected growth targets (that is, amount of growth per instructional week).
- Monitor progress over time.

The Hasbrouck & Tindal Oral Reading Fluency Data will give you information that will help you determine fluency goals for your students.

Hasbrouck & Tindal Oral Reading Fluency Data

Grades	Percentile	Fall WCPM*	Winter WCPM*	Spring WCPM*	Avg. Weekly Improvement**
1	90	–	81	111	1.9
	75	–	47	82	2.2
	50	–	**23**	**53**	**1.9**
	25	–	12	28	1.0
	10	–	6	15	0.6
2	90	106	125	142	1.1
	75	79	100	117	1.2
	50	**51**	**72**	**89**	**1.2**
	25	25	42	61	1.1
	10	11	18	31	0.6
3	90	128	146	162	1.1
	75	99	120	137	1.2
	50	**71**	**92**	**107**	**1.1**
	25	44	62	78	1.1
	10	21	36	48	0.8
4	90	145	166	180	1.1
	75	119	139	152	1.0
	50	**94**	**112**	**123**	**0.9**
	25	68	87	98	0.9
	10	45	61	72	0.8
5	90	166	182	194	0.9
	75	139	156	168	0.9
	50	**110**	**127**	**139**	**0.9**
	25	85	99	109	0.8
	10	61	74	83	0.7

(Continued)

(Continued)

Grades	Percentile	Fall WCPM*	Winter WCPM*	Spring WCPM*	Avg. Weekly Improvement**
6	90	177	195	204	0.8
	75	153	167	177	0.8
	50	**127**	**140**	**150**	**0.7**
	25	98	111	122	0.8
	10	68	82	93	0.8
7	90	180	192	202	0.7
	75	156	165	177	0.7
	50	**128**	**136**	**150**	**0.7**
	25	102	109	123	0.7
	10	79	88	98	0.6
8	90	185	199	199	0.4
	75	161	173	177	0.5
	50	**133**	**146**	151	**0.6**
	25	106	115	124	0.6
	10	77	84	97	0.6

Source: Copyright © 2005. Behavioral Research and Teaching. All rights reserved. This publication, or parts thereof, may not be used or reproduced in any manner without written permission.

*WCPM = Words Correct Per Minute

**Average weekly improvement is the average words per week growth you can expect from a student.

Example: Identify goal and timeline

Academic

BUNKY: EIGHTH-GRADE STUDENT

Reading Level = 94 wcpm, fourth grade

Benchmark for 8th grade = 133 wcpm

Necessary Gain = 39 wcpm

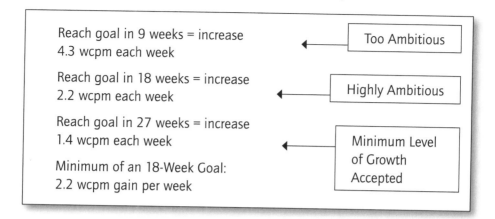

Behavioral Goal

MY TURN

GARY

Establish a Goal for Gary

- Gary is capable of doing accurate work; however, he completes 50 percent or less of required assignments. It is expected that Gary would complete 80 percent of his assignments with at least 80 percent accuracy.

- Write a goal for Gary (include time frame, materials, setting, students name, behavior, and criterion).

In nine weeks, Gary will complete 80 percent of his assignments with at least 80 percent accuracy in all of his classes as measured by teacher grade books.

YOUR TURN

EFFECTIVE PROBLEM SOLVING: INDIVIDUALS–ACTIVITY 13

Using information from the completed ICEL/RIOT form, establish a goal for Mary Ann. Be sure to include the elements of required for a measurable goal.

> *The greatest danger for most of us is not that our aim is too high and we miss it, but that it is too low and we reach it.*
>
> —Michelangelo

Step 4: Research-Based Intervention

Interventions are directly applied and result in an increase in skill or performance. An in-depth discussion of intervention is provided in Chapter 2. The information below is intended to highlight considerations for tailoring interventions for individual students.

Interventions are

- **linked to a goal.** The behavior or performance will change relative to the goal set by the team.
- **systematic and planned.** The procedures to be applied are specified clearly and completely.
- **validated** in scientific research.
- **applied directly**. They bring about improved performance.

Examples of Interventions

- Using a reading program that is corrective
- Teaching the student how to initiate peer interaction
- Instructing in following directions
- Using strategies for sentence writing
- Teaching strategies for test taking
- Providing positive reinforcement for behavior correction

Remember: Interventions are NOT

- accommodations;
- adaptations;
- interagency referrals;
- special education settings;
- assessments, evaluations, or screenings;
- classroom observations;
- advice or consultations;
- assisting with instructional methods and materials; or
- places.

Consider... How well do you understand interventions? Which of the following are interventions?

- Student attends resource room for reading.
- Student is taught how to divide single-digit problems.
- Teacher requests the student be evaluated for ADD.
- Student is referred for testing with the psychologist.
- Student is observed in the classroom.
- Student is reinforced for sitting in her seat.

Interventions should consist of the following instructional features:

- Direct and explicit instruction
- Multiple repetitions
- Modeling
- Guided/controlled opportunities for practice
- Constant checks on mastery
- Scaffold learning
- Corrective and immediate feedback

Team Process for Developing an Intervention for Individual Students

If problem analysis and the subsequent problem-solving steps have been completed, the intervention should be relatively straight forward. The following steps are often used to identify how the intervention will be carried out. Interventions created for individual students more often require time and resources not readily available within the existing tiered support structure within a school.

Problem solving for individual students can be accomplished through a team process using the following steps:

1. **Brainstorm.** Identify possible ideas for meeting the identified goal. Discourage evaluating or conversation about the ideas presented by participants. The goal is to elicit ideas within a specified time frame of four to six minutes.

2. **Clarify.** Ask whether any ideas need clarification and let the author of the question provide the clarification. Observe the questioner

during clarification and stop the clarification when the questioner indicates nonverbally or otherwise that he or she understands.

3. **Advocate.** Participants may advocate for as many ideas or combination of ideas as they wish. Statements of advocacy should be phrased positively. Advocate for the ideas that have the best chance of meeting the identified goal. Establish a "whatever it takes" mentality.

4. **Canvass.** Ask individuals in the group to identify a few ideas (between two to four) they think are most important. The ideas do not need to be in rank order. Take a hand count to determine which ideas are of greatest interest to the group.

YOUR TURN

MARY ANN

Develop an intervention for Mary Ann.

- Using the team process for developing an intervention, identify a research-based intervention for Mary Ann.
- Brainstorm
- Clarify
- Advocate
- Canvass

Step 5: Act on the Plan

Now the team needs to

- develop a plan to implement the intervention,
- ensure that whatever is necessary to carry out the intervention is available (resources, instructional time, expertise, training, etc.),
- identify how best to implement the intervention (when, whom, setting, etc.), and
- anticipate and develop a backup plan: Plan B.

A goal without a plan is just a wish.

When problem solving, remember that if problem analysis is performed properly, what needs to be taught will be straightforward. Providing that instruction, however, is more difficult because it often requires more than what is readily available within the existing tiered system of supports.

How do we write the implementation component? The implementation component is the blueprint or plan for implementing the intervention. Again, use a "whatever it takes" philosophy.

- Decide *what* steps and sequence need to be taken in order to implement the intervention plan.
- Decide and record *when* each step should be completed.
- Decide and record *who* will be responsible for carrying out each part of the intervention.

Dan's Implementation Plan

What will be done?	When	By Whom?
Corrective Reading	Daily 60 minutes	Mr. Means
Firm up	Daily 20 minutes in afternoon	Mrs. Smart
Six-Minute Solution	Daily 10 minutes	Mr. Means

Plan B: Add additional 45 minutes to Corrective Reading for preteach and reteach.

YOUR TURN

Effective Problem Solving: Individuals—Activity 14

- Assume you identified a sixth-grade student who requires an additional half hour of *Corrective Reading* per day as part of her intervention.
- Brainstorm possible ways, within your existing system, to provide an additional half hour for a double dose.

Step 6: Monitor the Plan

An intervention plan is not complete without a way to evaluate its effectiveness. Progress monitoring requires tracking (1) pacing, (2) content learning or in-program performance, and (3) out-of-program performance (such as DIBELS).

A graph is often the best way to show data because it is often easier to interpret data in this form. It creates a picture of learning to document results. It helps make decisions and predict outcomes.

Example: Basic Monitoring Graph

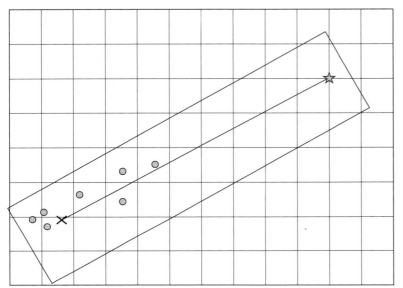

Consider identifying a range of acceptable behavior (RAB). The RAB is established by identifying both a highly ambitious rate of growth—the upper line—and a minimal of acceptable performance—the lower line of the RAB. Performance within the two lines represents acceptable performance. Three consecutive scores above or below the RAB should be given consideration for making a change to the intervention or goal.

WHAT RULES CAN I USE FOR MAKING DECISIONS?

- **Option I:** Moving Median*

   The decision is made when three consecutive data points fall above or below the aimline.

- **Option II:** Three-Day

   The decision is made after three data points (medians).

---

*Each data point will always be a median score.

Option I: Moving Median Data Decision Rules

1. If three consecutive data points are above the aimline, raise the criteria.

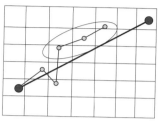

2. If three consecutive data points are below the aimline, change the intervention.

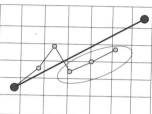

3. If the data points align with the aimline, the student is making adequate progress toward the benchmark goal.

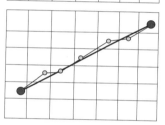

Option II: Three Day (Medians) Data Decision Rules

In this option, after an aimline is drawn, medians are plotted on the graph and three data points are used to tell whether the individual is achieving as predicted.

1. If three consecutive data points are above the aimline, raise the criteria.

2. If three consecutive data points are below the aimline, change the intervention.

3. If neither of the above rules applies, make no change.

Things to Consider Regarding Decision Making

- Focus on the question, "Will the individual reach his or her goal by the end of the goal period?"
- Decide to change the intervention whenever the rate of progress falls below the expectation.
- Think of changes to the intervention as fine tuning (alterable variables) rather than as major reconstruction of interventions.

Example: Three Day

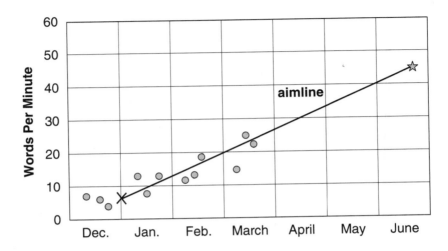

Changes in Intervention

1. Draw a phase line. A phase line is drawn vertically on the graph to identify the point at which the intervention change occurs.

2. Establish a new aimline. Find the median of the last three to five data points to establish a new baseline. Connect the new baseline median point to the goal.

Example: Phase Line

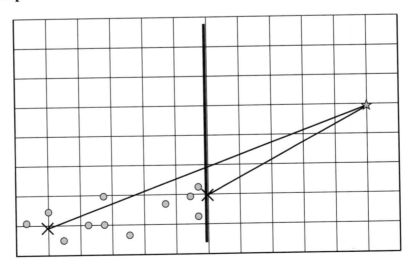

EVALUATING STUDENT PROGRESS: WHAT TO CONSIDER WHEN STUDENTS AREN'T LEARNING ENOUGH

Before changing interventions, consider these four questions:

1. Are we teaching the right things and using the best approach and/ or program?

2. Are we covering enough content to allow students to make expected progress toward closing the achievement gap?

3. Are students mastering what is being taught—are they learning it?

4. Are student generalizing acquired skills?

Additional Considerations for Improving Student Progress

1. *Alterable Variables*

2. *Consider the 5 Mores (Robinson, March 2009)*

- More explicit, direct instruction
- More modeling
- More practice with . . .
- More feedback
- More time

3. *What do we do when students aren't learning enough?*

We have an obligation to think of students as difficult to teach before we label them as unable to learn.

—Fletcher, Coulter, Reschly, & Vaughn, 2004

Alterable Variables Chart

Alterable Components	Specific Adjustments				
Opportunities to Learn (Time and/or Concentration of Instruction)	Increase attendance.	Provide instruction daily.	Increase opportunities to respond.	Vary schedule of easy and difficult tasks and skills.	Add another instructional period.
Program Efficacy	Preteach components of core program.	Use extension of core program.	Supplement core with appropriate materials.	Replace current core program.	Implement specially designed program.
Program Implementation	Model lesson delivery.	Monitor implementation frequently.	Provide coaching and ongoing support.	Provide additional staff development.	Vary program and/or lesson schedule.
Grouping for Instruction	Check group placement.	Reduce group size.	Increase teacher-led instruction.	Provide individual instruction.	Change instructor.
Coordination of Instruction	Clarify instructional priorities.	Establish concurrent reading periods.	Provide complementary reading instruction across periods.	Establish communication across instructors.	Meet frequently to examine progress.

Source: Oregon Reading First Center, Center on Teaching and Learning, Portland, OR.

Evaluate Progress and Adjust Instruction

"What to Do When Students Aren't Learning Enough"

STUDENT VARIABLES

_____ 1. Does the learner have a potential undiagnosed hearing or vision problem?

_____ 2. Is the learner frequently absent during reading instruction?

Decision Point: Do student variables potentially explain the learner's lack of progress?

YES   NO

If yes, specify a plan to address student factors.

_____ Check hearing and vision

_____ Develop systematic plan with parents to increase attendance

_____ Other

OPPORTUNITIES TO LEARN

_____ 1. Student was present 95 percent or more of instructional days.

_____ 2. Instruction was delivered five days per week.

_____ 3. Small-group teacher-directed instruction was conducted a minimum of thirty to forty-five minutes daily.

_____ 4. Student had frequent opportunities to respond to tasks during teacher-directed instruction.

Decision Point: Is Opportunity to Learn a potential factor explaining the learner's lack of progress?

YES   NO

If yes, specify a plan to increase Opportunity to Learn.

_____ Plan to increase attendance

_____ Add another instructional period daily

_____ Ensure instruction is provided daily

_____ Increase teacher-directed instruction (determine whether this is the appropriate group for the learner)

_____ Increase number of opportunities for learner to respond

---

Evidence of Program Efficacy

_____ 1. Does the instructional program have established and trustworthy evidence of effectiveness?

_____ 2. Do program components have evidence of effectiveness?

Decision Point: Is Program Efficacy a potential factor explaining the learner's lack of progress?

YES   NO

If yes, specify a plan to intensify Program Efficacy.

_____ Replace current core program

_____ Supplement program with appropriate materials (Please specify)

_____ Preteach core program

Implementation of Instruction

_____ 1. Is instruction implemented with a high level of fidelity?

_____ 2. Is an entire lesson and all its parts delivered daily?

_____ 3. Do learners respond accurately and often?

_____ 4. Are there lesson components on which instructor needs staff development?

Decision Point: Is Implementation of Instruction a potential factor explaining the learner's lack of progress?

YES   NO

If yes, specify a plan to intensify Implementation of Instruction.

_____ Provide additional staff development

_____ Model lesson delivery

_____ Replace current program

_____ Supplement program with specific materials (Please specify)

_____ Teach to mastery

Grouping for Instruction

_____ 1. Are students grouped based on instructional performance (i.e., Do students have similar instructional needs?)?

_____ 2. Are some students making significant progress and others not?

_____ 3. Are the lowest performers taught in the smallest group (e.g., 4–6 students)?\

_____ 4. Are the lowest performers taught by a strong, experienced, and well-qualified instructor?

_____ 5. Is student assignment to a group flexible, dynamic, and anchored to performance?

Decision Point: Is Grouping for Instruction a potential factor explaining the learner's lack of progress?

YES   NO

If yes, specify a plan to intensify Quality of Instruction.

_____ Subdivide group

_____ Reduce # of students in group

_____ Change instructor

_____ Other

Coordination/Alignment of Instruction

_____ 1. Are instructional priorities well understood and emphasized across all instructional settings?

_____ 2. Is concurrent reading instruction coordinated across instructional settings?

_____ 3. Are students receiving two periods of reading instruction in the same or complementary materials?

_____ 4. Is a system in place facilitating communication between general and special educators?

Decision Point: Is Coordination/Alignment of Instruction a potential factor explaining the learner's lack of progress?   YES   NO

If yes, specify a plan to intensify Quality of Instruction.

(Need to develop)

_____ Clarify instructional priorities

_____ Establish concurrent reading periods/sessions

_____ Provide complementary reading instruction across reading periods

_____ Establish a communication system

Progress Before Change to the Intervention

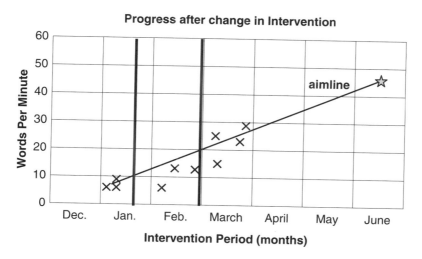

Progress after change in Intervention

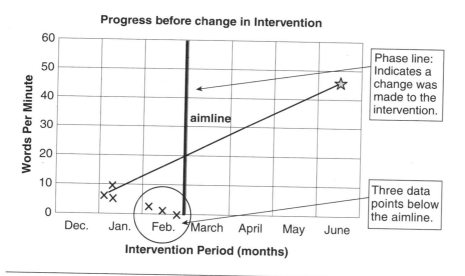

Progress before change in Intervention

Source: Oregon Reading First, Center on Teaching and Learning (CTL), University of Oregon.

KEYS TO SUCCESS

Remember

- Maintain a sense of urgency.
- Identify a specific goal and timeline.
- Use research-based interventions (with tenacity).
- Progress monitor to inform instruction (avoid insanity).
- Focus on alterable components.
- Keep a "Whatever it takes!" attitude.

YOUR TURN

EFFECTIVE PROBLEM SOLVING: INDIVIDUALS—ACTIVITY 15

1. Review the intervention plan you've created for Mary Ann and complete any unfinished portions of the plan.

2. Create a progress-monitoring graph for Mary Ann.

Blank worksheets and user forms discussed in this chapter are available for download at **www.partnersforlearning.org**.

RTI and Special Education Eligibility

7

OBJECTIVES:

- Understand key concepts for using RTI for special education identification
- Know the time frame for carrying out interventions as part of RTI
- Be able to explain the concept of adequate progress and its importance to eligibility decision making
- Understand why system effectiveness is critical if RTI is to be used for special education eligibility decision making
- Understand the required components to include in a comprehensive evaluation report

Response to Intervention is the practice of providing high-quality instruction and intervention matched to student need, monitoring progress frequently to make decisions about change in instruction or goals and applying child response data to important educational decisions.

—Batsche et al., 2005

The chapters leading up to this final chapter on Special Education Eligibility have detailed a systems standard protocol approach to RTI that, if well established, can prevent many students from ever needing to be considered for Special Education. Indeed, Response to Intervention at the secondary level is designed to ensure schools are well prepared to meet the needs of a diverse student population, including those with severe skill deficits. Both system-level interventions and individual student problem-solving efforts will likely meet the needs of most students. When students do not respond enough to Intensive-level interventions, special education may be necessary and is a logical, final means to serve students whose needs cannot be met through regular education support structures alone. This final chapter details how information collected, while providing interventions, can be used for the purpose of conducting a comprehensive evaluation and determining eligibility and need for special education.

Few decisions in education are as important and potentially life altering as the decision whether to place a student in special education. Consider the following:

- Sixty percent of all students in special education are those with specific learning disabilities (SLD).
- Up to eighty percent of SLD students are there because they haven't learned to read.
- Students in special education have
  o less exposure to regular education curricula and have fewer regular education friends, and
  o academic achievement is no better than that of similar but non-identified students.
- Few students in special education ever close the achievement gap.
- Few students exit special education.
- Placement in special education is a life-altering event. (President's Commission, 2002)

Special education is necessary and can be beneficial for students with disabilities. It should not, however, be used as a means of providing students academic and behavioral interventions that should be available through regular education. When this happens, special education is less effective for the truly disabled students because it attempts to serve curriculum casualties created by the shortcomings in regular education.

Although referrals to special education typically occur in elementary school, referrals at the secondary level often reflect limited viable options for struggling students; despite referrals, very few learning disabilities are diagnosed in middle and high school.

It is important to sound the reminder that special education entitlement is *not* the purpose of RTI. Rather, RTI is a means to prevent unnecessary placements and, in some cases, the need for even considering special education. RTI's purpose is to

- maximize and support student achievement,
- support teachers and parents or guardians,
- facilitate problem resolution, and
- provide interventions in the least restrictive way possible.

RTI PARADIGM SHIFT

The transition from a test-and-place, categorical, special-education-will-fix-them mentality to an RTI approach is difficult for reasons beyond learning new testing and determining eligibility practices. As outlined in previous chapters, RTI requires nothing short of rethinking and restructuring entire school systems, including assessment, structures of supports, schedules, intervention and instructional practices, using data for decision making, and so on.

Despite all the changes required for RTI, none is as important as the accompanying paradigm shift necessary to ensure that new and effective practices do not end with the same results. Indeed, if RTI simply becomes the new way to qualify students for special education, little will have been gained or accomplished.

In considering the paradigm shift necessary for effective RTI implementation, it is important to remember that

- student problems can be defined and changed,
- questions will drive assessments,
- assessments will inform instruction and be low inference, and
- enabled learning rather than discrepancy or diagnosis is the goal.

In the words of Rueda and Windmueller (2006), "the argument is not that the amount of specialized expertise and assistance provided to students should be decreased or disappear, as urban schools are filled with students who need meaningful assistance. Rather we argue that the assistance needs to be more closely targeted to the underlying (validated, not presumed) causes." To achieve this goal, research points clearly to Applied Behavior Analysis, Progress Monitoring, and Direct Instruction as an integral part of addressing student needs both in and out of special education (Forness, Kavale, Blum, & Lloyd, 1997).

USING RTI FOR SPECIAL EDUCATION ELIGIBILITY DECISIONS

For schools or districts considering using RTI for special education eligibility decisions, a common question is where to start. Individual states are either in the process of or already have developed guidelines for schools to follow in using RTI for eligibility decisions. IDEA provided the following guidance to states (U.S. Department of Education, 2013, Section 300.307 Specific Learning Disabilities):

- States must not require the use of a severe discrepancy between intellectual ability and achievement for determining whether a child has a specific learning disability.
- States must permit the use of a process based on the child's response to scientific, research-based intervention.

Before detailing how an RTI process can be applied for making eligibility decisions, several additional considerations are in order.

Is RTI Optional?

Although schools or districts can choose to continue using an IQ/achievement approach to determine eligibility for specific learning disabilities, the essential elements of RTI are not optional. Consider the following IDEA regulation requiring LEAS as part of the evaluation:

- Prior to, or as part of the referral process, the child was provided appropriate instruction and intervention by qualified personnel in regular education settings.
- Data-based documentation of repeated assessments of achievement at reasonable intervals, reflecting formal assessment of student progress during instruction, was provided to the child's parents. (U.S. Department of Education, 2013, Code 300.309)

> IDEA regulation states: "If a child has not made adequate progress after an appropriate period of time . . . a referral for an evaluation to determine if the child needs special education and related services must be made."

What Is the Time Frame for Carrying Out Interventions as Part of RTI?

The time frame for carrying out intervention is not defined in IDEA regulation, meaning there is no time frame for carrying out or completing intervention. The timeline for completing an evaluation begins "once the child is referred for an evaluation . . . " (U.S Department of Education, 2013, Code 300.309). Operationalized, the intervention period could be interpreted that as long as adequate progress is evident, interventions instead of special education consideration could be continued indefinitely. It should be noted, however, that RTI cannot be used to delay a comprehensive evaluation if a student is suspected of having a disability.

A general timeline for evaluating the effects of an intervention is as follows:

- 30 minutes per day
- 3–5 times per week
- 8–16 weeks
- Reliable progress (slope) evaluation typically requires sixteen data points.

> IDEA regulation also specifies that "once the child is referred for an evaluation to determine if the child needs special education and related services, the timeline described in 300.301 and 300.303 must be adhered to, unless extended by mutual written agreement of the child's parents and a group of qualified professionals." (U.S. Department of Education, 2013, Code 300.309)

In other words, the timeline for completing an evaluation once it is initiated is finite and defined by IDEA regulation. The timeline for initiating an evaluation, however, is indefinite and determined by the referral team based on continued examination of a student's progress throughout the course of intervention. Ideally, the decision to move to evaluation for special education should be made when the referral team can substantiate that (1) all reasonable efforts to address the problem have been exhausted and (2) despite multiple interventions carried out with fidelity for sufficient time periods, the student's progress is insufficient as measured by

a. progress or growth of typical peers,

b. progress or growth of similar students receiving the same or similar interventions, and

c. the need for intervention and accommodation is necessary for an indefinite period of time based on the trend line of the student's demonstrated progress.

What Is Adequate Progress?

Also not specified by IDEA regulation is the definition of adequate progress. Without clear guidance, a definition of *adequate progress* may be academic growth that is generally consistent with the progress of similar performing students. This requires the use of formative measures that not only evaluate a student's progress but also establish a standard for growth based on similar peers in the particular area of interest. The graph below illustrates how a student is compared to the growth of similarly skilled peers.

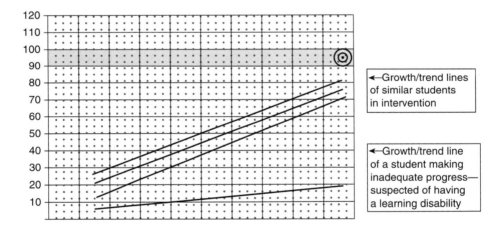

The second graph below illustrates the distinction between adequate and inadequate progress. Lines A and B represent the trajectory of growth for Intensive students who are making adequate progress. The data trend reveals that with time and continued intervention, both students will close the achievement gap and will, in the foreseeable future, move out of Intensive-level status. Line C, on the other hand, illustrates the trajectory of a student who, despite some progress, will remain in the Intensive status well into the foreseeable future. This progress illustrates a student who is not closing the achievement gap and will require intervention for an indefinite time period.

Focus on Trajectory

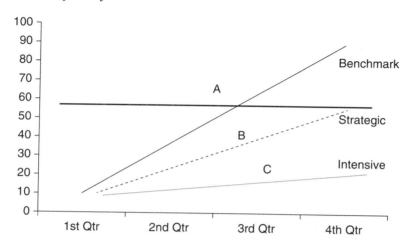

KEY CONSIDERATIONS FOR APPLYING
RTI TO SPECIAL EDUCATION ELIGIBILITY DECISIONS

RTI, as an alternative to the ability achievement discrepancy approach, offers powerful advantages: namely, more accurate identification, more accurate eligibility determination after intervention efforts, and the provision of instructionally relevant information for mapping a future plan for intervention and support. Despite these and other advantages, RTI must be carried out with a high degree of precision to maximize its true potential. Key considerations include the following:

- Ensuring the effectiveness of the system (tiered supports)
- Structuring interventions for success—such as having adequate amount of time in intervention each day
- Identifying accurate expectations for growth (timeline and rate or amount of improvement)
- Using meaningful and sensitive measures of student growth (progress monitoring)
- Clearly defining how much response is enough or defining clear goals for improvement prior to evaluating response to intervention

1. Effectiveness of Systems

Evaluating systems effectiveness is discussed at length in Chapter 5, but its importance cannot be over-emphasized. Without healthy systems at all levels (Benchmark, Strategic, Intensive), student difficulty may simply be a symptom of broader, non-student-related problems. For instance, if interventions are not accurately implemented, are inadequately matched to student needs, or suffer from any number of execution pitfalls, student casualties will result. In this scenario, students end up being referred to special education because of system rather than student failure. Systems must be constantly evaluated to ensure a high degree of effectiveness to prevent over-referral and the resulting over-placement in special education.

2. Structure Interventions for Success

Considerations for interventions are also discussed in Chapter 5. Here are key considerations to maximize intervention effectiveness:

- Interventions should be initiated early and carried out with fidelity.
- Interventions should not be an afterthought or considered a "quick fix."
- Consideration should be given to thinking of intervention as a *second or alternate to a core class*. Too often intervention is fragmented and provided in addition to core classes, which may actually cause more harm than good, especially if students fail classes for which they are capable of passing. Example: a 7th grade student with 2nd grade math skills are likely better served in an intervention class matched to his or her instructional level (but accelerated) rather than placed in a 7th grade math class plus an additional period for intervention.
- Interventions should be goal oriented—designed to achieve well-defined outcomes.
- Pacing is critical—schools should identify what and how much needs to be taught to allow students to catch up.
- Amount of time in intervention should be based on how much time is necessary to cover and master identified daily learning objectives or lessons.
- Double dose and triple dose if additional instructional time is necessary to ensure mastery or firming up of daily learning objectives. Additional doses can allow students to keep up with pacing goals established at the onset of intervention.
- Consideration should be given to in-program and out-of-program performance of students. Remember, nothing has been taught until something has been learned—and retained!

3. Identify Accurate Expectations for Growth

Using a student's response to intervention as part of eligibility for special education requires establishing accurate expectations for growth. Goals that are overly ambitious will result in faulty decision making. Likewise, goals that are not ambitious enough may likely be achieved, but will contribute to a student's lack of overall progress. In both instances, eligibility decisions would be distorted and faulty.

To identify accurate expectations, consider the following:

- What is the outcome goal?
- What is the student's present level of performance?
- How much growth and time is required?
- How much growth is required per week to meet the outcome goal?

The example below illustrates how expectations for growth and timeline can be calculated. The student's growth is compared to the weekly improvement of typical students to ensure realistic and ambitious progress is established. Established expectations will be used for decision making regarding intervention effectiveness as well as student response to intervention.

Identify Goal and Timeline

(ACADEMIC)

Bunky: Eighth Grade

Reading Level = 65 wpm, Sixth Grade

Benchmark for Eighth Grade = 146 wpm

Necessary Gain (wpm) = <u>66</u>

9 wks = 8.8	←	Too Ambitious
18 wks = 4.4	←	Highly Ambitious
27 wks = 2.96	←	Realistic

Establish a 27 Week Goal: 2.96 wpm per week

2005 Hasbrouck & Tindal Oral Reading Fluency Data

Jan Hasbrouck and Gerald Tindal completed an extensive study of oral reading fluency in 2004. The results of their study are published in a technical report entitled, "Oral Reading Fluency: 90 Years of Measurement," which is available on the University of Oregon's website, brt.uoregon.edu/tech_reports.htm.

This table shows the oral reading fluency rates of students in Grades 1 through 8 as determined by Hasbrouck and Tindal's data.

You can use the information in this table to draw conclusions and make decisions about the oral reading fluency of your students. **Students scoring below the 50th percentile using the average score of two unpracticed readings from grade-level materials need a fluency-building program.** In addition, teachers can use the table to set the long-term fluency goals for their struggling readers.

Average weekly improvement is the average words per week growth you can expect from a student. It was calculated by subtracting the fall score from the spring score and dividing the difference by 32, the typical number of weeks between the fall and spring assessments. For Grade 1, since there is no fall assessment, the average weekly improvement was calculated by subtracting the winter score from the spring score and dividing the difference by 16, the typical number of weeks between the winter and spring assessments.

Grade	Percentile	Fall WCPM*	Winter WCPM*	Spring WCPM*	Avg. Weekly Improvement**
1	90		81	111	1.9
	75		47	82	2.2
	50		23	53	1.9
	25		12	28	1.0
	10		6	15	0.6
2	90	106	125	142	1.1
	75	79	100	117	1.2
	50	51	72	89	1.2
	25	25	42	61	1.1
	10	11	18	31	0.6
3	90	128	146	162	1.1
	75	99	120	137	1.2
	50	71	92	107	1.1
	25	44	62	78	1.1
	10	21	36	48	0.8
4	90	145	166	180	1.1
	75	119	139	152	1.0
	50	94	112	123	0.9
	25	68	87	98	0.9
	10	45	61	72	0.8
5	90	166	182	194	0.9
	75	139	156	168	0.9
	50	110	127	139	0.9
	25	85	99	109	0.8
	10	61	74	83	0.7
6	90	177	195	204	0.8
	75	153	167	177	0.8
	50	127	140	150	0.7
	25	98	111	122	0.8
	10	68	82	93	0.8

Grade	Percentile	Fall WCPM*	Winter WCPM*	Spring WCPM*	Avg. Weekly Improvement**
7	90	180	192	202	0.7
	75	156	165	177	0.7
	50	128	136	150	0.7
	25	102	109	123	0.7
	10	79	88	98	0.6
8	90	185	199	199	0.4
	75	161	173	177	0.5
	50	133	146	151	0.6
	25	106	115	124	0.6
	10	77	84	97	0.6

*WCPM=Words Correct Per Minute

**Average words per week growth

4. Use Meaningful and Sensitive Measures of Student Growth

Formative assessments that are meaningful and sensitive to student progress allow accurate decision making. The value of curriculum-based measurement in concert with in-program assessment is outlined in earlier chapters of this manual. Together, along with teacher judgment, these measures provide a comprehensive picture of student progress, providing insight into two important questions:

1. Are students learning what is being taught?

2. Are they generalizing acquired skills for application in academic and real-life situations?

DETERMINATION OF SPECIAL EDUCATION ENTITLEMENT

Special education entitlement is based on two elements: need and eligibility.

Need requires determining in a specific, systematic manner whether progress has been made and whether that progress would continue to be made without special education services. This can be accomplished by examining the student's response to intervention: acquisition rate, retention rate, and resources necessary to support the student's need.

Eligibility requires determining in a specific, systematic manner whether the discrepancy between the individual's performance and the expected performance is severe enough to require resources beyond general education.

Dual Discrepancy Eligibility Criteria

The dual discrepancy criterion does not rely on discrepancy between innate ability and academic performance. Rather, students may be placed according to a severe discrepancy in initial skill level and growth, as illustrated below.

Dual Discrepancy: Severely Discrepant in Initial Skill Level and Growth

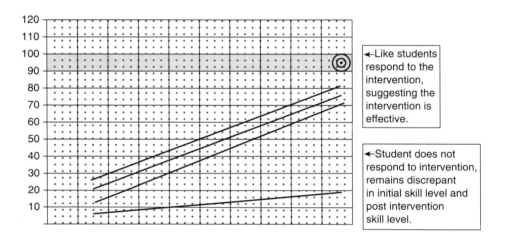

Dual discrepancy is defined as follows:

- Student exhibits large differences from expected levels of performance in achievement, social behavior, or emotional regulation.
- There is evidence of insufficient response to high-quality interventions in academic and/or behavioral domains of concern.

Example Indicators

Source	Criteria
1. Curriculum-Based Measurement (CBM) score comparing a student to grade-appropriate benchmark *(The criterion for a significant discrepancy is a median score that is at or below the 7th percentile on materials from one grade level below the student's current placement.)*	7th percentile or lower

Source	Criteria
2. Standardized Assessment *(A transformed standard score that is at or greater than 1.75 standard deviations from the mean of the general education peer comparison.)*	1.75 or more standard deviation (SS = 74 or fewer)
3. Discrepancy Ratio *(A discrepancy ratio is determined by taking the expected criterion and dividing it by the student's current performance. The criterion for a significant discrepancy ratio for each grade level is 2.0 or greater.)*	2.0 or greater
4. Instructional placement two or more grade levels below actual grade placement *(Performance that falls two or more years below the current grade placement is considered significant.)*	Two grade levels Below grade placement

Above indicators must be supported by other documentation, including performance on state assessments, classroom performance, placement in intervention, and so on.

Look at the Individual's Response to Intervention: What Happened?

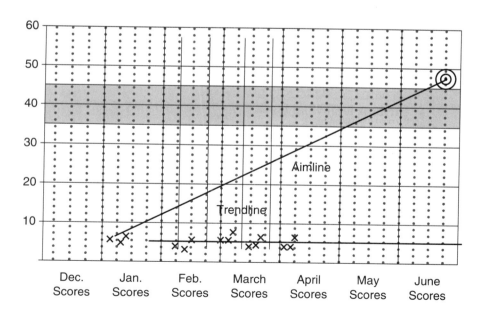

Consider the Rate of Acquisition

- to help determine whether the individual is learning at the expected rate (closing the achievement gap),
- to help determine the need for continued intervention,
- to evaluate the effectiveness of intervention, and
- to help determine the need for changes in the intervention or the criteria.

Consider the Rate of Retention

- to help determine whether the individual will be successful in the general education setting,
- to help determine the ability of the individual to retain and use the information or skills,
- to help determine the need for ongoing support or structured learning,
- to help determine the ability of the individual to generalize the information or skills learned,
- to help determine possible need for long-term accommodations, and
- to help determine the individual's need for extended-year special education services.

REQUIRED ELEMENTS TO INCLUDE IN A COMPREHENSIVE EVALUATION REPORT

A student may not be considered eligible for special education if not provided appropriate instruction or if the difficulty is due to limited English proficiency.

Difficulties cannot be due to

- visual, hearing, or motor disability,
- mental retardation,
- emotional disturbances,
- cultural factors,
- environmental or economic disadvantage, or
- limited English proficiency.

Reports must show

- background information;
- an indication that an opportunity to learn was provided;

- that student skills deficits were resistant to well-implemented, research-based intervention;
- that a student's skills are significantly below expectation; and
- that deficits were not due to exclusionary factors.

EXAMPLE: ELIGIBILITY CRITERIA FOR APPLYING RTI TO ELIGIBILITY DECISIONS

Consider the following questions:

1. Is there evidence of a lack of response to intervention? In other words, did the student's response to intervention remain substantially below that of other students in the same instructional group receiving similar interventions? Did the student's performance fail to significantly improve despite meaningful and periodic changes to the interventions carried out for a considerable length of time (for example, 16–24 weeks)?

2. What resources are necessary to support the child to participate and progress in the general education curriculum? Describe the supports necessary and why regular education is not able to provide the particular student's educational needs.

3. Is there a dual discrepancy evident in the student's performance in the area(s) of concern? The discrepancy must be documented in terms of initial skill level as well as growth during intervention. See possible indicators of data supporting a dual discrepancy.

4. Does the evidence collected empirically support the team's decision for special education placement? In other words, can the team verify that the interventions were research-based, well implemented, and the student's performance well documented so the team feels confident in the decision made?

IEP VS. EFFECTIVE RTI APPROACH: WHY PLACEMENT?

What changes can we expect once a student is placed on an Individual Education Program (IEP) compared to interventions available through an effective RTI approach? Regarding intervention, hopefully, there would be no changes. If more effective intervention or instruction is available through special education, the student's intervention should be reevaluated. Rather than qualifying a student for special education to bring about an intervention that is otherwise not available in regular education, RTI teams should ask what intervention is necessary and how to make it available for any and all students—no IEP required.

The role of an IEP is to ensure that a student, once identified as eligible and in need of special education, has access to the general education curriculum and is provided the appropriate learning opportunities, accommodations, adaptations, specialized services, and supports the student needs to progress toward the learning standards.

An IEP addresses the following:

- Formalizes the plans that are made for the student.
- States the educational goals for the student.
- States the modified learning outcomes, any adaptations, and/or special materials.
- Describes the services that are to be provided for the student.
- Provides a focus for collaborative planning among the various people who are involved with the student.

RTI's Impact on Special Education

Although RTI is a regular education function, its impact to special education is significant. An RTI approach will impact special education regarding

- when students are placed in special education,
- how students are identified (eligibility),
- what professionals do,
- who gets special education services, and
- focus of service.

YOUR TURN

SPECIAL EDUCATION ENTITLEMENT—ACTIVITY 16

As a group, discuss

1. What advantages and disadvantages can you identify using a dual discrepancy approach to eligibility versus a traditional IQ/achievement discrepancy approach?

2. Using the RTI Implementation Checklist, evaluate your school's readiness for using a Response to Intervention approach to special education eligibility. What components are in place, partially in place, or not in place? Identify goals and actions to address the areas identified as not in place. (See RTI Implementation Checklist, page 143.)

CONCLUSION

This chapter presented information for using RTI as a means of determining special education eligibility. It detailed specific considerations that must be accounted for in order for RTI to be used accurately for special education decision making. Although the purpose of RTI is not to provide a new and improved method for identifying students as learning disabled, thoughtful implementation of its practices will certainly make such decisions more accurate and special education less likely to be overused as a means of providing otherwise unavailable support to students.

> Approach special education with greater creativity and flexibility. . . . Instead of engaging in polarizing discussions around whether to mainstream students versus serve them in pullout settings—or around the disproportionate identification of students by race—let's focus on how to differentiate learning for *all* students . . . How we can make education "special" for every one of our students, reserving unique services for the small percentage of severely disabled children who need them? (Scull & Winkler, 2011, p. 16)

"*When we know better, we do better.*"

Maya Angelou

Blank worksheets and user forms discussed in this chapter are available for download at **www.partnersforlearning.org**.

References

Allensworth, E., & Easton, J. Q. (2005). *The on-track indicator as a predictor of high school graduation*. Chicago, IL: Consortium on Chicago School Research. Retrieved from http://ccsr.uchicago.edu/publications/track-indicator-predictor-high-school-graduation

Archer, A. (2007). *Active participation: Engaging them all*. National Reading First Comprehension Conferences, St. Louis, MO.

Baker, S. K., Simmons, D. C., & Kame'enui, E. J. (1995). *Vocabulary acquisition: Synthesis of the research*. Technical report No. 13 for the National Center to Improve the Tools of Educators, University of Oregon. Retrieved from http://www.doe.virginia.gov/instruction/virginia_tiered_system_supports/training/higher_ed/vocab_acquisition_synthesis_of_research.pdf

Batsche, G. (2006). *Problem solving and response to intervention: Implications for state and district policies and practices*. Retrieved from http://www.casecec.org/powerpoints/rti/CASE%20Dr.%20George%20Batsche%201-25-2006.ppt

Batsche, G., Elliott, J., Graden, J. L., Grimes, J., Kovaleski, J. F., Prasse, D., et al. (2005). *Response to intervention: Policy considerations and implementation*. Alexandria, VA: National Association of State Directors of Special Education.

Beck, I., McKeown, M., & Kucan, L. (2002). *Bringing words to life: Robust vocabulary instruction*. New York: Guilford.

Biemiller, A. (2004). Teaching vocabulary in the primary grades: Vocabulary instruction needed. In J. Baumann & E. Kame'enui (Eds.), *Vocabulary instruction: Research to practice* (pp. 28–40). New York: Guilford.

Denton, C. A. (n.d.). *High-quality classroom instruction, classroom reading instruction that supports struggling readers*. Houston: Children's Learning Institute, University of Texas Health Science Center Houston. Retrieved from http://www.rtinetwork.org/essential/tieredinstruction/tier1/high-quality

Denton, C. A., Fletcher, J. M., Simos, P. C., Papanicolaou, A. C., & Anthony, J. L. (2007). An implementation of a tiered intervention model: Reading outcomes and neural correlates. In D. Haager, J. Klingner, & S. Vaughn (Eds.), *Evidence-based reading practices for response to intervention* (pp. 107–137). Baltimore, MD: Brookes.

Eaker, R., DuFour, R., & DuFour, R. (2002). *Getting started: Reculturing schools to become professional learning communities.* Bloomington, IN: National Educational Service.

Education Week, Children Trends Database, researched January 1, 2014. Retrieved from http://www.childtrends.org/databank/

"Ellis & Worthington. (1995)." is a citation in "Hall, T. (n.d.). *Explicit Instruction: Effective classroom practices report.*" published by the "National Center on Accessing the General Curriculum" found at http://www/cast.org/system/galleries/download/ncac/ExpInstrucNov2.pdf

Feldman, K., & Kinsella, K. (2005). Narrowing the language gap: The case for explicit vocabulary instruction. Scholastic Professional Paper. Retrieved from http://teacher.scholastic.com/products/authors/pdfs/narrowing_the_gap.pdf

Fixsen, D. L., & Blasé, K. A. (2009, January). *Implementation: The missing link between research and practice.* NIRN Implementation Brief #1. Chapel Hill: The University of North Carolina, FPG, NIRN.

Fixsen, D., Naoom, S., Blasé, K., Friedman, R., & Wallace, F. (2005). *Implementation research: A synthesis of the literature.* Tampa: University of South Florida.

Fletcher, J. M., Coulter, W. A., Reschly, D. J., & Vaughn, S. (2004, December). Alternative approaches to the definition and identification of learning disabilities: Some questions and answers. *Annals of Dyslexia, 54*(2), 304–331.

Flugum, K. R., & Reschly, D. J. (1994). Pre-referral interventions: Quality indices and outcomes. *Journal of School Psychology, 32,* 1–14.

Forness, S. R., Kavale, K. A., Blum, I. M., & Lloyd, J. W. (1997). What works in special education and related services: Using meta-analysis to guide practice. *Teaching Exceptional Children, 29*(6), 4–9.

Francis, D. J., Shaywitz, S. E., Stuebing, K. K., Shaywitz, B. A., & Fletcher, J. M. (1996). Developmental lag versus deficit models of reading disability: A longitudinal, individual growth curves analysis. *Journal of Educational Psychology, 88,* 3–17.

Fullan, M. (2003). *Change forces with a vengeance.* New York, NY: Routledge.

Fullan, M. G. (1991). *The new meaning of education change.* New York, NY: Teachers College Press.

Fullan, M., & Quinn, J. (2010). *Capacity building for whole system reform.* Retrieved from http://www.michaelfullan.ca/media/13435862150.html

Garmston, R. J., & Wellman, B. M. (2002). *The adaptive school: A sourcebook for developing collaborative groups.* Lanham, MD: Rowman & Littlefield.

Graves, K. (2000). *Designing language courses: A guide for teachers.* Boston, MA: Heinle & Heinle.

Hasbrouck, J., & Tindal, G. A. (2005). Oral reading fluency: 90 years of measurement. Eugene: Behavioral Research and Teaching at University of Oregon. Retrieved from http://www.brtprojects.org/publications/dl/51

Marzano, R. J. (2004). The developing vision of vocabulary instruction. In J. F. Baumann & E. J. Kame'enui (Eds.), *Vocabulary instruction: From research to practice* (pp. 100–117). New York: Guilford.

Mathes, P. G., & Denton, C. A. (2002). The prevention and identification of reading disability. *Seminars in Pediatric Neurology, 9*(3), 185–191.

Medina, J. (2008). *Brain rules: 12 principles for surviving and thriving at work, home, and school.* Seattle, WA: Pear Press.

Meyers, C., & Jones, T. (1993). *Promoting active learning. Strategies for the college classroom.* San Francisco, CA: Jossey-Bass.

National Center on Response to Intervention. (2007). *RTI practices glossary.* Retrieved from http://www.rti4success.org/index.php?option=com_content&task=view&id=634&Itemid=2

National Center on Response to Intervention. (2012, November). *Using fidelity to enhance program implementation within an RTI framework handouts & references.* Washington, DC: U.S. Department of Education, Office of Special Education Programs.

Oregon Reading First, Center on Teaching and Learning. (n.d.) Eugene: University of Oregon. Retrieved from http://oregonreadingfirst.uoregon.edu

Petrosini, L., Graziano, A., Mandolesi, L., Neri, P., Molinari, M., & Leggio, M. G. (2003). Watch how to do it! New advances in learning by observation. *Brain Research Reviews, 42,* 252–264.

Pondiscio, R. (2012, October 8). Demographics isn't destiny [Web log post]. Retrieved from http://blog.coreknowledge.org/author/robert-pondiscio/page/2/

President's Commission. (2002). *President's commission on excellence in special education.* Washington, DC: U.S. Government Printing Office. Retrieved from http://www.gpo.gov/fdsys/pkg/CHRG-107shrg80787/html/CHRG-107shrg80787.htm

Robinson, J. (2009, March). Oregon Reading First: Cohort B Leadership Session. Oregon Reading First Center, Center on Teaching and Learning, Portland, OR.

Rosario, R. (2010). *Troubled youths get a message of hope.* St. Paul, MN: Pioneer Press. Retrieved from http://www.twincities.com/ci_16599369?source=email&nclick_check=1

Rosenshine, B., & Stevens, R. (1986). Teaching functions. In M. Wittrock (Ed.), *Handbook of research on teaching* (3rd ed., pp. 376–391). New York: Macmillan.

Rueda, R., & Windmueller, M. P. (2006, March). English language learners, LD, and overrepresentation: A multiple-level analysis. *PRO-ED Journals.* Retrieved from http://www.redorbit.com/news/education/432469/english_language_learners_ld_and_overrepresentation_a_multiple_level_analysis/

Ryan, R., & Deci, E. (2000). Self-determination theory and the facilitation of intrinsic motivation, social development, and well-being. *American Psychologist, 55*(1), 68–78.

Scammacca, N., Roberts, G., Vaughn, S., Edmonds, M., Wexler, J., Reutebuch, C. K., & Torgesen, J. K. (2007). *Intervention for adolescent struggling readers: A meta-analysis with implication for practice.* Portsmouth, NH: RMC Research Corporation, Center on Instruction. Retrieved from http://www.rti4success.org/sites/default/files/coi_struggling_readers.pdf

Scull, J., & Winkler, A. M. (2011, May). *Shifting Trends in Special Education.* Retrieved from http://www.edexcellencemedia.net/publications/shifting-trends-in-special.html

Stahl, S. A., & Fairbanks, M. M. (1986). The effects of vocabulary instruction: A model-based meta-analysis. *Review of Educational Research, 56*(1), 72–110.

Sugai, G. (2007). *RTI: Reasons, practices, systems, & considerations.* Storrs: University of Connecticut. Retrieved from http://www.pbis.org/common/pbisresources/presentations/gsrtikeynote1207.ppt

Tackett, K. K., Roberts, G., Baker, S., & Scammaca, N. (2009). *Implementing response to intervention: Practices and perspectives from five schools. Frequently asked questions.* Portsmouth, NH: RMC Research Corporation, Center on Instruction.

Tindal, G. A., Shinn, M. R., Walz, L., & Germann, G. (1987). Mainstream consultation in secondary settings: The Pine County model. *Journal of Special Education, 21*(3), 94–106. doi: 10.1177/002246698702100308

Torgesen, J. K. (2004). Lessons learned from research on interventions for students who have difficulty learning to read. In P. McCardke & V. Chhabra (Eds.), *The voice of evidence in reading research* (pp. 355–382). Baltimore, MD: Brookes.

U.S. Department of Education. (2010). *The nation's report card: Reading 2009* (NCES 2010–458). Washington, DC: U.S. Government Printing Office, National Center for Education Statistics.

U.S. Department of Education. (2013). *The nation's report card: A first look: Reading 2013* (NCES 2014–451). Washington, DC: U.S. Government Printing Office, National Center for Education Statistics.

Index

CORWIN
A SAGE Company

The Corwin logo—a raven striding across an open book—represents the union of courage and learning. Corwin is committed to improving education for all learners by publishing books and other professional development resources for those serving the field of PreK–12 education. By providing practical, hands-on materials, Corwin continues to carry out the promise of its motto: **"Helping Educators Do Their Work Better."**